THE CHOLA EMPIRE
Legends of the Indian Ocean

THE CHOLA EMPIRE

Legends of the Indian Ocean

Parthasarathy G

All rights reserved.
Copyright © 2022 by Parthasarathy G

While every effort has been made to trace copyright holders and obtain permission, this has not been possible in all cases; any omissions brought to our attention will be remedied in future editions.

No Part of this book may be reproduced or transmitted in any form or by any means, electronic or mechanical, including photocopying, recording, or by any information storage and retrieval system, without the prior written permission of the copyright owner.

For information Email:sarathy1210@yahoo.co.in

Dedicated to all history enthusiasts and lovers of the past...

CONTENTS
ACKNOWLEDGEMENTS
INTRODUCTION
MARITIME TRADITIONS: FOUNDATIONS OF CHOLA NAVAL SUPREMACY
RAJENDRA CHOLA'S AMBITIONS
RAJENDRA CHOLA'S CAMPAIGN AGAINST SRIVIJAYA
TEMPLE ARCHITECTURE AND ART
ADMINISTRATION AND GOVERNANCE
TRADE AND DIPLOMACY
CULTURAL EXCHANGE
LEGACY AND IMPACT

ACKNOWLEDGEMENTS

Thank you, dear reader and friend, for choosing to read **"The Chola Empire: Legends of the Indian Ocean "**.

I would like to express my gratitude to everyone who supported me in writing this book.

First and foremost, I would like to thank Rahul, my first reader, for his invaluable feedback.

I would also like to thank my friends and family who have made life worth living. A special shoutout to my extended family on Instagram, Twitter, and Facebook for their constant support.

Last but not least, I want to express my appreciation to the entire team at NotionPress Publications and Amazon kdp for their hard work in bringing this book to life.

Welcome to **"The Chola Empire: Legends of the Indian Ocean"**. I hope you enjoy reading it as much as I enjoyed writing it.

◆ ◆ ◆

INTRODUCTION

In the annals of history, the Chola Empire stands as a testament to the heights of South Indian civilization. From the 9th to the 13th centuries, the Cholas forged an empire that encompassed vast territories in present-day Tamil Nadu, parts of Andhra Pradesh, Kerala, and even reached as far as Sri Lanka, the Maldives, and Southeast Asia. Renowned for their administrative acumen, artistic patronage, and maritime achievements, the Cholas left an indelible mark on the cultural, economic, and political landscape of the region.

At the height of their power, the Cholas established a kingdom that rivaled any contemporary empire. Their capital, Thanjavur (formerly known as Tanjore), flourished as a center of trade, art, and learning. Under the patronage of the Chola rulers, a remarkable fusion of Tamil culture, Sanskrit traditions, and influences from neighboring regions flourished, giving rise to a unique Chola identity.

The Chola era witnessed an unparalleled cultural renaissance. Literature, poetry, and drama thrived, with celebrated works like the epic poem "Silappatikaram" and the collection of hymns known as the "Tevaram." The

Cholas' love for the arts extended to music and dance, as evidenced by the intricate sculptures adorning their temples depicting graceful dancers and musicians. Temple rituals, religious festivals, and devotional practices formed an integral part of Chola society, with the magnificent "Brihadeeswarar Temple" in Thanjavur serving as a testament to their architectural and spiritual grandeur.

The Chola period is often hailed as the golden age of temple architecture. The Chola kings and their patrons left behind a rich architectural legacy characterized by towering gopurams, intricately carved pillars, and majestic stone sculptures. The magnificent temples of "Gangaikonda Cholapuram", "Darasuram", and "Brihadeeswarar Temple" showcase the Chola dynasty's architectural prowess and their devotion to deities. These architectural marvels not only exemplify the skill of the Chola craftsmen but also provide insights into the religious and social fabric of Chola society.

The Chola Empire thrived due to its flourishing economy, built upon robust agricultural practices and vibrant trade networks. The fertile river valley of the Kaveri River allowed for bountiful harvests, sustaining a prosperous agrarian society. Trade played a pivotal role in the Chola economy, with a well-developed maritime network connecting the ports of South India with distant lands. Merchants traversed the Indian Ocean, carrying valuable commodities such as spices, textiles, gems, and precious metals, thereby creating a vibrant economic ecosystem.

What truly set the Cholas apart was their maritime prowess. The Chola navy, equipped with formidable warships, dominated the seas and ensured the security of trade routes. The strategic location of ports like Kaveripattinam (Puhar) and Nagapattinam facilitated thriving maritime trade with Southeast Asia, China, the Arabian Peninsula, and even East Africa. The Chola naval expeditions, led by visionary rulers like Rajendra Chola I, extended the empire's influence to foreign lands, establishing Chola outposts and fostering cultural exchanges that left an indelible impact on regional dynamics.

The Chola Empire's rise to power was not merely the result of military conquest but also an embodiment of a vibrant and prosperous civilization. The Cholas' cultural and economic achievements, coupled with their architectural splendor and naval supremacy, cemented their legacy as one of the most remarkable dynasties in Indian history. As we embark on a journey through the annals of Chola history, we will explore their accomplishments, delve into the intricacies of their trade networks, marvel at their artistic heritage, and witness the grandeur of their maritime expeditions. Let's uncover the remarkable story of the Cholas and their conquest of the seas.

MARITIME TRADITIONS: FOUNDATIONS OF CHOLA NAVAL SUPREMACY

Before the Cholas embarked on their extraordinary naval expeditions, they stood on the shoulders of a rich maritime heritage that had flourished in the region for centuries. The ancient seafaring traditions of South India laid the foundation for the Chola Empire's naval supremacy, influencing their navigational techniques, shipbuilding prowess, and trade networks. In this chapter, we will dive into the depths of these maritime traditions, uncovering the secrets of the sea that propelled the Cholas to conquer the waves.

The Chola region, known for its vibrant seafaring culture, owes its maritime prowess to a variety of geographical advantages. These natural blessings, including a long coastline, abundant rivers, and a strategic location along key trade routes, played a significant role in shaping the Chola Empire's relationship with the sea and their remarkable achievements in navigation and trade.

Firstly, the Chola region boasts a remarkable coastline that stretches for miles along the Bay of Bengal. The mesmerizing beauty of the sandy beaches and the rhythmic waves crashing against the shore instilled a sense of adventure in the hearts of the Chola people. The long coastline provided abundant opportunities for fishing, fostering a close connection between the Cholas and the bounty of the sea. Moreover, the coastline served as a gateway to the vast ocean, beckoning the Cholas to embark on daring voyages of exploration and trade.

The rivers of the Chola region were another crucial factor in nurturing the seafaring culture. These rivers, such as the Kaveri, Vaigai, and Palar, not only brought life-giving water to the fertile lands but also acted as natural highways, connecting the inland areas to the coast. The Cholas harnessed the navigable routes offered by these rivers, facilitating the movement of goods and fostering trade. The rivers became lifelines of connectivity, linking the agricultural heartland to the bustling coastal towns and ports, further enriching the maritime culture of the Chola Empire.

In addition to the coastline and rivers, the strategic location of the Chola region played a vital role in its seafaring culture. Situated at the crossroads of major trade routes, the Chola Empire became a central hub for maritime trade between various regions. Merchants from Southeast Asia, the Arabian Peninsula, and even

East Africa converged upon the Chola ports, seeking to tap into the prosperity and opportunities offered by this strategic location. The Cholas, in turn, capitalized on their advantageous position, establishing diplomatic relations, and expanding their influence across the seas.

The strategic location of the Chola region also made it a gateway to the wealth and exoticism of the East. It served as a crucial link between India and Southeast Asia, enabling cultural, commercial, and diplomatic exchanges. The Cholas developed strong connections with the kingdoms of Southeast Asia, fostering a vibrant trade network and sharing knowledge, ideas, and customs. These connections not only enriched the maritime ambitions of the Chola Empire but also influenced their art, architecture, and religious practices.

The seafaring culture of the Chola region flourished due to its geographical advantages. The long coastline, numerous rivers, and strategic location along key trade routes provided the Chola Empire with abundant resources, connectivity, and opportunities for trade and exploration. These geographical blessings nurtured a vibrant maritime culture, enabling the Cholas to become a dominant naval power in their era. The legacy of the Cholas' seafaring traditions continues to captivate our imagination, reminding us of the remarkable achievements made possible by the unique geographical advantages of the region.

The ancient texts and archaeological findings provide us with valuable insights into the early evidence of maritime activities and the deep-rooted connection that the people of the Chola region had with the sea.

In the ancient texts, such as the Tamil Sangam literature, we find references to the sea as a vital element of the Chola society. These texts depict the sea as a source of livelihood, adventure, and cultural exchange. They mention the bravery and skills of the Chola seafarers, who ventured into the vast ocean in search of new lands, trade opportunities, and glory.

Archaeological discoveries further confirm the long-standing maritime connection of the Chola people. Excavations conducted at sites like Arikamedu, Nagapattinam, and Kaveripattinam (Puhar) have unearthed remnants of ancient ports, dockyards, and maritime infrastructure. These findings include remnants of ancient vessels, pottery, anchors, and maritime equipment, providing tangible evidence of the Chola people's engagement in maritime activities.

The presence of trade-related artifacts, such as Roman coins, Chinese ceramics, and exotic goods from Southeast Asia, suggests the existence of vibrant maritime trade networks. These findings not only showcase the Chola Empire's involvement in trade but also highlight their role as intermediaries in connecting different regions through maritime routes.

The depiction of maritime scenes in ancient art and temple sculptures further emphasizes the importance of the sea in Chola society. Sculptures found in temple complexes portray maritime activities, including sailors navigating ships, merchants trading goods, and maritime deities blessing the seafarers. These artistic representations provide visual evidence of the integral role that maritime activities played in the lives and beliefs of the Chola people.

The presence of navigational knowledge and terminology related to the sea in ancient Tamil literature and inscriptions also indicates the Chola people's familiarity with maritime activities. The precise descriptions of wind patterns, navigation techniques, and the use of stars for celestial navigation reflect the depth of their understanding of the ocean and its challenges.

Collectively, the ancient texts, archaeological findings, artistic representations, and navigational knowledge provide compelling evidence of the Chola people's long-standing connection with the sea. They highlight the maritime heritage that shaped the Chola Empire's seafaring culture and set the stage for their remarkable achievements in navigation, trade, and maritime dominance.

The early evidence of maritime activities in ancient texts and archaeological findings serves as a testament to the enduring relationship between the Chola people and the sea. It is a reminder of their rich maritime heritage, their spirit of exploration, and their contribution to the maritime history of the region.

The Adventurous Spirit of the Mariners:

Let's embark on a journey to discover the bold and adventurous spirit of the ancient Chola mariners during the Chola period. These courageous sailors went beyond the familiar shores, venturing into unknown territories, and establishing trade links that stretched across vast distances.

The Chola mariners possessed an unwavering spirit of exploration. Driven by curiosity and a thirst for discovery, they set sail into the vast ocean, ready to face the challenges that lay ahead. Their courageous hearts propelled them towards distant lands, where new opportunities awaited.

In the heart of the Chola Empire, ancient ports like Kaveripattinam, also known as Puhar, bustled with maritime activity. These vibrant harbors became the gateway to the vast ocean, attracting merchants and seafarers from distant lands. Here, the Chola mariners set sail on their magnificent vessels, venturing forth into the unknown with the determination to unravel the secrets of the seas.

As their ships sailed across the waves, the Chola mariners encountered numerous trading settlements along their journey. They ventured to places like Nagapattinam, where bustling markets and vibrant exchanges brought together merchants from various corners of the world. In these trading settlements, the Chola mariners interacted with traders from faraway lands, forging economic ties, and exchanging valuable goods that enriched the Chola Empire's prosperity.

The maritime explorations of the Chola mariners extended beyond the shores of their own kingdom. They navigated their way to neighboring regions, leaving their mark in the annals of history. The Chola mariners set foot on the shores of Sri Lanka, establishing strong maritime connections and fostering cultural exchanges between the two lands. They traded not only goods but also ideas, beliefs, and customs, further strengthening the bond between these neighboring regions.

Further afield, the Chola mariners ventured into Southeast Asia, where they encountered kingdoms such as Srivijaya and Sailendra. These interactions led to the establishment of thriving trade networks, connecting the Chola Empire with the wealth and exoticism of the East. The Chola mariners brought back treasures from these distant lands, enriching their own society and introducing their people to new wonders.

These intrepid sailors braved the unpredictable seas, guided by their knowledge of the winds, stars, and currents. With their sturdy ships and skilled navigation techniques, they charted new routes and opened up unexplored horizons. Their determination knew no bounds as they pushed the boundaries of their known world, driven by the desire to expand their influence and build prosperous trade networks.

As they ventured into unknown waters, the Chola mariners encountered diverse cultures and encountered foreign lands. They embraced the richness of these new lands, establishing trade links and fostering cultural exchanges. Through their interactions, they shared knowledge, goods, and ideas, enriching their own society while leaving a lasting impact on the lands they visited.

The Chola mariners played a crucial role in connecting distant regions. Their fearless spirit and willingness to explore enabled them to establish trade links that spanned vast distances. They brought back exotic goods from faraway lands, introducing their people to new treasures and expanding the horizons of Chola society.

In their pursuit of trade and exploration, the Chola mariners became ambassadors of their empire. Their presence in foreign lands not only fostered economic prosperity but also strengthened diplomatic ties. They showcased the Chola Empire's influence and power, leaving an indelible mark wherever they sailed.

The bold and adventurous spirit of the ancient Chola mariners continues to inspire us today. Their remarkable journeys remind us of the power of curiosity, determination, and the human spirit's unyielding thirst for exploration. Their legacy serves as a testament to the indomitable courage and resilience of those who dare to venture beyond familiar shores in search of new horizons.

The tales of Chola's early maritime explorations are filled with awe-inspiring encounters, remarkable achievements, and the spirit of adventure. They highlight the Chola Empire's maritime prowess, as well as their commitment to expanding their influence beyond their own borders. These maritime explorations laid the foundation for vibrant trade networks, cultural exchanges, and diplomatic ties that shaped the course of history.

The legacy of the Chola mariners' early maritime explorations serves as a reminder of the indomitable spirit of exploration and the enduring connections forged through trade and interaction. Their journeys continue to captivate our imaginations, painting a vivid picture of a bygone era when the Chola Empire's ships sailed across the seas, carrying the hopes and dreams of a civilization that dared to explore the unknown.

Celestial Navigation Knowledge

In ancient times, when Chola seafarers embarked on their voyages across the vast Indian Ocean, they relied on various methods to navigate their way through the open waters. One such method, known as celestial navigation, played a crucial role in guiding them on their maritime journeys.

Celestial navigation involved observing and studying the celestial bodies, such as the sun, stars, and constellations, to determine the position and direction of their ships. Chola seafarers understood that these celestial bodies followed predictable patterns in the sky, which could be used as navigational aids.

During the daytime, the sun served as a valuable reference point for Chola mariners. By observing the sun's position in the sky, they could determine the direction in which they were sailing. For example, if the sun was directly overhead, it meant they were sailing towards the east. If it appeared on the horizon, it indicated a westward direction. This knowledge of the sun's movement allowed them to chart their course and stay on the right path.

At night, the Chola seafarers turned their attention to the stars and constellations. They recognized certain star patterns that remained constant throughout the year, such as the North Star, also known as Polaris. By observing the position of Polaris in relation to other stars, the mariners could determine their latitude or how far north or south they were from a reference point. This information was crucial for plotting their course accurately.

In addition to Polaris, Chola seafarers studied other prominent stars and constellations that appeared in the night sky. They could identify specific constellations, such as the Big Dipper or Orion, and use their positions to navigate. By tracking the movement of these stars over time, the mariners could estimate their own ship's direction and adjust their course accordingly.

Celestial navigation required knowledge, experience, and a keen eye for observing the sky. Chola seafarers developed a deep understanding of celestial bodies and their movements, which allowed them to navigate confidently across the Indian Ocean.

By harnessing the power of celestial navigation, the Chola mariners were able to sail vast distances, explore new lands, and establish trade networks with distant regions. Their expertise in using celestial bodies as navigational aids played a significant role in their maritime achievements and contributed to the Chola Empire's dominance in the Indian Ocean.

The knowledge and techniques of celestial navigation passed down by the Chola seafarers paved the way for future generations of navigators, leaving an enduring legacy in the history of maritime exploration.

Knowledge of Monsoon Winds

In ancient times, the Chola Empire's seafarers possessed a remarkable understanding of the monsoon winds and their crucial role in maritime trade and travel. These seasonal winds played a vital role in shaping their voyages, and the Cholas mastered the art of harnessing their power for safe and efficient journeys.

The monsoon winds were strong and predictable winds that blew across the Indian Ocean during specific times of the year. The Cholas recognized that these winds could either aid or hinder their maritime endeavors, and thus, they carefully planned their voyages around the changing monsoon seasons.

The Chola mariners understood that the monsoon winds consisted of two primary seasons: the Southwest Monsoon and the Northeast Monsoon. The Southwest Monsoon brought winds blowing from the southwest, while the Northeast Monsoon brought winds blowing from the northeast. These seasonal shifts in wind direction were crucial for the success of their voyages.

During the Southwest Monsoon season, the Chola mariners took advantage of the winds blowing towards the northeast. They set sail from their home ports, such as Kaveripattinam, and embarked on their journeys to distant lands, including Southeast Asia. The Southwest Monsoon winds propelled their ships, making their voyages faster and more efficient.

As the season transitioned to the Northeast Monsoon, the winds changed direction, blowing from the northeast. The Chola mariners used this knowledge to plan their return journeys. They harnessed the power of the Northeast Monsoon winds to sail back to their home ports, completing their voyages and ensuring a safe return.

The Cholas' understanding and mastery of the monsoon winds gave them a significant advantage in maritime trade and travel. They timed their departures and arrivals to coincide with the favorable monsoon seasons, ensuring smooth and efficient navigation across the Indian Ocean.

Utilizing the monsoons required careful planning and navigational expertise. The Chola mariners closely observed the changes in wind patterns and planned their voyages accordingly. They studied the behavior of the monsoon winds over generations, passing down this invaluable knowledge from one seafarer to another.

By harnessing the power of the monsoon winds, the Chola mariners facilitated extensive trade networks, connecting the Chola Empire with distant lands. They transported goods, ideas, and cultures across vast distances, contributing to the empire's prosperity and influence.

The Cholas' understanding and mastery of the monsoon winds stand as a testament to their expertise in navigating the seas and their ability to adapt to the natural elements. Their knowledge of these winds not only shaped their maritime endeavors but also left a lasting impact on the history of trade and travel in the Indian Ocean region.

Ancient Shipbuilding Techniques

Let's take a fascinating journey into the ancient shipbuilding techniques of the Chola Empire, where skilled craftsmen showcased their remarkable expertise in constructing sturdy and seaworthy vessels. These ships played a crucial role in facilitating long-distance travel and trade, and their construction methods and unique features were awe-inspiring.

The craftsmen of ancient South India employed a range of materials to build their ships. They primarily used sturdy timber, such as teak and jackfruit wood, renowned for their durability and resistance to water. These woods were carefully selected for their strength, allowing the ships to withstand the challenges of the open seas.

The construction of Chola ships involved intricate techniques and meticulous attention to detail. The craftsmen used wooden planks, expertly joined together using a technique known as "mortise and tenon." This method involved creating slots (mortises) in one piece of wood and fitting them with protruding parts (tenons) on another piece, creating a secure and strong connection. This ensured that the ships remained watertight and structurally sound.

One of the unique features of Chola ships was their flexibility. The craftsmen built the ships with a slight curve, known as "hogging," which helped them navigate through rough waters. This design allowed the ships to withstand the powerful forces of the sea, ensuring their seaworthiness even during storms.

To make the ships even more resilient, the craftsmen employed caulking techniques. They filled the gaps between the wooden planks with materials like coconut fiber or tar, creating a watertight seal. This caulking prevented water from seeping into the ship, adding an extra layer of protection against the harsh elements of the sea.

Chola ships were also equipped with advanced rigging systems that allowed for effective navigation and control.

They featured multiple masts and sails, which could be adjusted to harness the power of the winds and propel the ships forward. These sails were expertly crafted from materials like cotton or silk, enabling the ships to glide smoothly through the water.

The ancient Chola ships were not only sturdy but also designed with spacious interiors. They had separate compartments for cargo storage, allowing for efficient trade and transportation of goods. These ships could carry a considerable amount of cargo, ensuring that the Chola Empire's trading ventures flourished.

The shipbuilding techniques of the Chola Empire showcased the extraordinary skills and craftsmanship of the ancient South Indian artisans. Their expertise in selecting suitable materials, constructing robust vessels, and incorporating unique features contributed to the success of Chola maritime trade and travel.

The Chola ships were renowned for their reliability, durability, and suitability for long-distance voyages. They played a vital role in connecting the Chola Empire with distant lands, fostering cultural exchanges and economic growth.

The legacy of the Chola's ancient shipbuilding techniques endures, reminding us of the remarkable achievements of these skilled craftsmen. Their ships, constructed with care and precision, sailed the vast seas, leaving a lasting impact on the history of maritime trade and travel.

Maritime Trade Routes:

The Chola Empire's maritime trade routes stretched far and wide, connecting South India with regions like Southeast Asia, China, the Arabian Peninsula, and East Africa. These routes formed a complex web of connections, facilitating the exchange of goods, ideas, and cultures between different lands.

One of the significant trade routes was the route that linked South India with Southeast Asia. Chola ships sailed across the Bay of Bengal, carrying goods to places like Srivijaya, Sailendra, and other kingdoms in Southeast Asia. This trade route allowed for the exchange of various commodities and fostered cultural interactions between the Chola Empire and the kingdoms of Southeast Asia.

Another important route led to China, where Chola traders sought to establish profitable trade connections. They navigated through the South China Sea, trading valuable goods like spices, textiles, and precious metals with the Chinese merchants. This trade route not only enriched the Chola Empire's coffers but also facilitated cultural exchanges between the two regions.

The Chola Empire's maritime trade routes also extended to the Arabian Peninsula, where they traded with the ports along the Red Sea and the Persian Gulf. The Chola mariners sailed across the Arabian Sea, carrying a wide range of goods like textiles, spices, and luxury items. These commodities were highly sought after in the markets of the Arabian Peninsula, and their trade contributed significantly to the economic prosperity of the

Chola Empire.

The maritime trade routes of the Chola Empire also reached the eastern coast of Africa, opening up avenues for trade with regions like present-day Kenya and Tanzania. Chola ships sailed along the Indian Ocean, transporting goods like textiles, spices, and precious metals. This trade facilitated interactions between the Chola Empire and the kingdoms of East Africa, paving the way for cultural exchange and economic growth.

The commodities traded along these maritime routes were diverse and valuable. The Chola Empire exported a wide range of goods, including spices like pepper, cinnamon, and cardamom, which were in high demand across various regions. Textiles, such as silk and cotton fabrics, were also traded extensively, showcasing the fine craftsmanship of the Chola artisans. Precious metals like gold and silver, as well as luxury goods like gemstones and ivory, added to the richness of the trade.

The significance of these commodities in fostering economic prosperity cannot be overstated. The trade in spices, textiles, precious metals, and luxury goods brought wealth and prosperity to the Chola Empire. It allowed the empire to accumulate wealth, establish strong diplomatic ties, and elevate its status as a dominant maritime power in the Indian Ocean.

The maritime trade routes of the Chola Empire were not merely commercial pathways but also conduits of cultural exchange and mutual understanding. They shaped the history and legacy of the Chola Empire, leaving an indelible mark on the trade networks of the Indian Ocean and contributing to the growth and richness of the civilizations that thrived along these routes.

Trading Hubs and Ports:

Let's explore the trading hubs and ports along the South Indian coastline during the time of the Chola Empire. These bustling centers of commerce and cultural exchange played a pivotal role in facilitating trade, accommodating foreign merchants, and establishing diplomatic relations.

One of the prominent trading hubs was Kaveripattinam, also known as Puhar. Located on the east coast of South India, Kaveripattinam served as a bustling port and a major center of trade during the Chola era. It was strategically positioned at the mouth of the Kaveri River, making it an ideal gateway for maritime commerce. Merchants from various regions, including Southeast Asia, China, Arabia, and East Africa, converged here to engage in trade with the Chola Empire. Kaveripattinam thrived as a cosmopolitan hub, fostering cultural exchanges and economic growth.

Nagapattinam was another significant port that played a crucial role in the Chola maritime trade. Situated on the Coromandel Coast, Nagapattinam served as a gateway for trade with Southeast Asian kingdoms. The port attracted merchants from distant lands, who arrived with their goods and exchanged them for the valuable commodities of the Chola Empire. Nagapattinam also served as a center for maritime activities, providing facilities for ship repairs, provisioning, and accommodations for visiting merchants.

Mamallapuram, also known as Mahabalipuram, was renowned for its architectural marvels and served as a vital trading hub during the Chola period. Located on the southeastern coast of South India, Mamallapuram had a strategic location along the trade routes of the Indian Ocean. The port attracted merchants and traders from different regions, who sought to engage in commerce with the Chola Empire. The exquisite stone carvings and sculptures of Mamallapuram stand as a testament to its historical significance as a center of trade and cultural exchange.

These trading hubs and ports served as vibrant and dynamic centers of commerce, accommodating foreign merchants and establishing diplomatic relations. They were equipped with marketplaces, warehouses, and docking facilities to facilitate trade activities. The Chola Empire welcomed foreign merchants, providing them with a conducive environment for conducting business and fostering diplomatic ties.

The ports acted as gateways for goods, ideas, and cultures to flow in and out of the Chola Empire. They played a crucial role in the exchange of commodities such as spices, textiles, precious metals, and luxury goods, which contributed to the economic prosperity of the Chola Empire. These trading hubs also served as cultural melting pots, where people from different regions interacted, shared knowledge, and forged new connections.

The importance of these trading hubs and ports along the South Indian coastline cannot be overstated. They were the lifeline of the Chola maritime trade, connecting the empire with distant lands and fostering economic growth and cultural diversity. The legacy of these trading hubs and ports continues to resonate in the history of maritime trade and cultural exchange in the Indian Ocean region.

RAJA RAJA CHOLA I

Raja Raja Chola I, also known as Raja Raja the Great, was a prominent ruler of the Chola Empire, which flourished in South India during the medieval period. Born in the 10th century CE, Raja Raja Chola I hailed from the illustrious Chola dynasty, known for its influential and powerful rulers.

Raja Raja Chola I ascended to the throne around the year 985 CE, following the demise of his father, Parantaka Chola II. His accession to power marked a crucial turning point in the history of the Chola Empire. While some rulers inherited the throne, Raja Raja's rise to power was the result of his military prowess and strategic acumen.

Under the reign of Raja Raja Chola I, the Chola Empire witnessed unprecedented expansion and cultural achievements. His military campaigns were instrumental in extending the Chola territories to encompass significant parts of South India, including Tamil Nadu, Kerala, Karnataka, and parts of Sri Lanka. Raja Raja Chola I's conquests earned him a formidable reputation as a skilled and ambitious ruler.

Beyond his military conquests, Raja Raja Chola I was a patron of arts, literature, and architecture. His reign witnessed a renaissance in the cultural and artistic spheres, with the construction of magnificent temples and the promotion of Tamil literature. The Brihadeeswarar Temple in Thanjavur, a UNESCO World Heritage Site, stands as a testimony to his architectural vision and grandeur.

Raja Raja Chola I's contributions to the Chola Empire's expansion and cultural achievements were transformative. His reign marked a golden age in the history of the Chola dynasty, characterized by political stability, economic prosperity, and cultural flourishing. The empire reached unprecedented heights of power and influence under his rule, leaving an indelible mark on South Indian history.

Raja Raja Chola I's enduring legacy extends beyond his military triumphs and architectural marvels. His reign is celebrated as a period of remarkable cultural and artistic achievements, shaping the identity and heritage of the Chola Empire. Today, his contributions are revered as a testament to the greatness and resilience of the Chola dynasty, solidifying his status as one of the most influential rulers in the history of South India.

Early Life and Ascendancy

Raja Raja Chola I's early life was marked by a nurturing environment that prepared him for the responsibilities of rulership. Born into the prestigious Chola dynasty, he received a comprehensive education, which included instruction in warfare, administration, and the arts.

From a young age, Raja Raja Chola I displayed a keen interest in governance and military strategies. He received guidance from renowned scholars and advisors who helped shape his understanding of statecraft and leadership. Alongside his intellectual pursuits, he underwent rigorous military training, honing his skills in combat and strategic warfare.

The circumstances surrounding Raja Raja Chola I's ascension to the throne were not without challenges. After the demise of his father, Parantaka Chola II, a power struggle ensued within the Chola Empire. Raja Raja Chola I emerged as a strong contender, displaying both his military prowess and his ability to garner support from influential nobles and courtiers.

With his charisma, astute political maneuvers, and military victories, Raja Raja Chola I successfully consolidated his power and emerged as the undisputed ruler of the Chola Empire. His ascent to the throne marked a crucial turning point, where his vision and ambition would shape the destiny of the empire.

During the early years of his reign, Raja Raja Chola I undertook significant efforts to establish his authority and leadership. He swiftly dealt with internal dissent and rebellion, ensuring stability within the empire. Through decisive military campaigns, he expanded Chola territories, subjugating rival kingdoms and extending Chola influence far and wide.

One notable achievement during his early reign was the successful naval expedition to Sri Lanka, where he defeated the powerful Mahinda dynasty and established

Chola dominance over the island. This victory not only showcased his military acumen but also solidified the Chola Empire's control over strategic maritime trade routes in the Indian Ocean.

Furthermore, Raja Raja Chola I's early reign witnessed the initiation of grand construction projects, including the iconic Brihadeeswarar Temple in Thanjavur. This architectural marvel, dedicated to Lord Shiva, served as a symbol of his power and devotion. The temple stands as a testament to his patronage of the arts and his vision for the empire's cultural renaissance.

Raja Raja Chola I's early reign was characterized by his ability to navigate complex political landscapes, consolidate power, and establish himself as a formidable leader. His strategic prowess, combined with his passion for governance and warfare, laid the foundation for his transformative reign. The early years of his rule demonstrated his determination to uphold the dignity and sovereignty of the Chola Empire, setting the stage for his remarkable achievements in the years to come.

Military Conquests

Raja Raja Chola I, renowned for his military prowess, embarked on several remarkable campaigns and conquests that expanded the boundaries of the Chola Empire and solidified its dominance in the region. Through strategic planning, innovative tactics, and sheer determination, he achieved unprecedented victories over rival kingdoms and extended Chola control over vast territories.

One of Raja Raja Chola I's notable military achievements was his successful campaign against the powerful Eastern Chalukya dynasty. The Eastern Chalukyas had long been a formidable adversary, but Raja Raja Chola I devised a meticulous strategy that involved both land and naval warfare. He led his troops in a series of decisive battles, ultimately emerging triumphant and capturing the territories of Vengi and Kanchi.

Another significant conquest under Raja Raja Chola I's leadership was the annexation of the Pandyan Kingdom. The Pandyas had posed a continuous threat to Chola sovereignty, and Raja Raja Chola I recognized the importance of subjugating this rival kingdom. Through a combination of military might, shrewd diplomacy, and covert operations, he defeated the Pandyas and incorporated their territories into the Chola Empire.

Raja Raja Chola I's military ambitions were not limited to the Indian subcontinent. He sought to extend Chola influence and control beyond the mainland, leading to his remarkable naval expedition to Sri Lanka. With an impressive fleet of warships and a skilled navy, Raja Raja Chola I defeated the reigning Mahinda dynasty and established Chola dominance over the island. This victory not only secured valuable resources and trade routes but also served as a testament to the Chola Empire's naval might and maritime supremacy.

Under Raja Raja Chola I's rule, the Chola Empire also witnessed significant territorial expansion in Southeast Asia. His military campaigns in regions such as Myanmar (Burma), Malaysia, and Indonesia led to the establishment of Chola vassal states and trade outposts. These conquests not only extended the influence of the Chola Empire but also facilitated cultural exchange and economic prosperity through maritime trade.

The Chola Empire's military successes were greatly facilitated by the establishment and development of a formidable naval fleet. Raja Raja Chola I recognized the strategic importance of maritime supremacy and invested heavily in naval infrastructure. He constructed numerous ports and harbors along the South Indian coastline, including the renowned port city of Nagapattinam. These ports served as vital hubs for trade, military operations, and the maintenance of a powerful naval fleet.

Raja Raja Chola I's naval fleet comprised advanced warships equipped with state-of-the-art technology and weaponry. The Cholas were pioneers in maritime engineering, with their ships featuring innovative design elements such as watertight compartments, advanced navigation systems, and even early versions of the keel. These technological advancements gave the Chola navy a significant edge over their adversaries, allowing them to project their military might across the Indian Ocean.

Through his military conquests, Raja Raja Chola I expanded the Chola Empire's territories, subdued rival kingdoms, and established the empire as a dominant maritime power. His victories showcased his strategic genius, organizational skills, and unwavering determination. The Chola Empire's military triumphs, both on land and at sea, contributed to its status as a formidable force in South Asia and left a lasting legacy in the annals of military history.

Legacy and Impact

Raja Raja Chola I's reign left a profound and lasting impact on the Chola Empire and the history of South India. His military conquests expanded the empire's territories and established Chola dominance, while his administrative reforms centralized governance and improved infrastructure. The architectural marvels he commissioned, such as the Brihadeeswarar Temple, showcased the empire's artistic brilliance. Raja Raja Chola I's influence extended beyond his reign, setting a precedent for subsequent rulers and shaping the cultural and political landscape of South India. His legacy continues to be celebrated for its contributions to Chola history, art, architecture, and governance.

RAJENDRA CHOLA'S AMBITIONS

Rajendra Chola was a significant ruler who reigned over the Chola Empire during a remarkable period in South Indian history. He came from an esteemed lineage and followed in the footsteps of his influential father, Rajaraja Chola I.

Rajendra Chola's journey began as he ascended to the throne, taking on the responsibilities of ruling a vast and powerful empire. His father, Rajaraja Chola I, had already established the Chola Empire as a prominent force in South India. Rajendra Chola inherited this legacy and aimed to continue the empire's growth and influence.

Being born into the Chola dynasty, Rajendra Chola was well aware of the rich heritage and achievements of his ancestors. His father's reign had set a high standard, marked by impressive architectural accomplishments, military triumphs, and advancements in trade and culture.

Rajaraja Chola, I had created a strong foundation for the empire, and his reign served as a significant influence on

Rajendra Chola's upbringing and development as a leader. The guidance and teachings of his father played a crucial role in shaping Rajendra Chola's ambitions and governing principles.

With a notable lineage and the knowledge passed down from his father, Rajendra Chola embarked on his reign with a sense of purpose and determination. He aimed to leave his mark on history and further expand the Chola Empire's power and influence.

Rajendra Chola's ascent to the throne marked a new chapter in the Chola Empire's history, one that would witness remarkable achievements and ambitions realized. His rule would be characterized by grand naval expeditions, territorial conquests, and an enduring legacy as one of the most influential Chola rulers.

Vision for Expansion

Rajendra Chola, a visionary ruler of the Chola Empire during the 11th century, harbored a strong ambition to extend Chola influence beyond the Indian subcontinent.

Rajendra Chola had a grand vision of expanding the reach and influence of the Chola Empire far beyond the shores of the Indian subcontinent. He recognized the strategic importance of establishing Chola dominance in the Indian Ocean region and sought to achieve this through a combination of naval power, control of the seas, and strategic thinking.

Understanding the significance of naval power, Rajendra Chola invested heavily in building a formidable navy. He recognized that control of the seas would be crucial in realizing his ambitions. By strengthening the Chola naval forces, he aimed to secure key trade routes, protect Chola interests, and project his authority over distant lands.

Rajendra Chola's emphasis on naval power allowed him to assert Chola dominance and establish control over regions that were vital for trade and strategic interests. He understood that a strong navy was not only crucial for defense but also instrumental in projecting Chola power and facilitating maritime trade, which would ultimately contribute to the economic prosperity of the empire.

In planning and executing his naval campaigns, Rajendra Chola demonstrated exceptional strategic thinking and organizational skills. He meticulously planned his expeditions, taking into account factors such as monsoon winds, trade routes, and the strengths and weaknesses of rival kingdoms. His strategic prowess allowed him to launch successful campaigns and achieve significant victories in distant lands.

Rajendra Chola's organizational skills were evident in his ability to mobilize and manage a large naval fleet. He ensured that his forces were well-equipped, trained, and coordinated, enabling them to execute complex naval maneuvers and effectively engage with enemy forces. His leadership and organizational acumen played a vital role in the success of Chola naval campaigns.

In summary, Rajendra Chola's ambition to extend Chola influence beyond the Indian subcontinent was fueled by his recognition of the importance of naval power, control of the seas, and strategic thinking. He invested in building a strong navy, strategically planned his campaigns, and demonstrated exceptional organizational skills. Through his vision and leadership, Rajendra Chola successfully expanded Chola influence, projecting their authority and achieving significant victories in distant lands.

Naval Strength and Strategies

During the rule of Rajendra Chola, the Chola navy experienced significant advancements, allowing the empire to assert its dominance over the seas.

Under the leadership of Rajendra Chola, the Chola navy underwent notable advancements, becoming a formidable force in the Indian Ocean. The empire invested in building a powerful fleet, equipped with sophisticated warships and manned by skilled mariners.

The Chola navy boasted an impressive array of warships, known as "Kappal" in the Tamil language. These warships were well-constructed and designed to withstand the challenges of long-distance travel and naval warfare. They were equipped with advanced navigation systems, weaponry, and defensive mechanisms, ensuring the safety and efficiency of Chola naval expeditions.

Skilled mariners formed the backbone of the Chola navy. They were highly trained in the art of sailing, navigation, and maritime warfare. Their expertise allowed them to effectively harness the power of the winds, navigate treacherous waters, and engage in naval battles with precision. The Chola mariners were known for their bravery, discipline, and unwavering loyalty to their ruler.

Rajendra Chola employed various naval strategies to

achieve his military objectives. One such strategy was the effective use of the monsoon winds. Rajendra Chola's forces meticulously planned their expeditions, taking advantage of the seasonal monsoons that swept across the Indian Ocean. By strategically timing their voyages, the Chola navy was able to harness the power of the winds, ensuring swift and efficient travel.

Another key naval strategy employed by Rajendra Chola was the coordination and synchronization of naval forces. He organized his fleet into different squadrons, each with a specific role and objective. This allowed for effective coordination during naval battles and ensured a well-organized approach to achieving military objectives.

Rajendra Chola also emphasized the importance of intelligence gathering and information networks. He established a network of spies and scouts who provided vital information on rival kingdoms, trade routes, and potential targets. This intelligence allowed him to plan his naval campaigns with precision, targeting vulnerable regions and exploiting the weaknesses of enemy forces.

Under Rajendra Chola's rule, the Chola navy experienced significant advancements. The empire's sophisticated warships and skilled mariners formed a formidable force in the Indian Ocean. Rajendra Chola employed naval strategies such as leveraging the monsoon winds, coordinating fleet movements, and prioritizing intelligence gathering. These efforts contributed to the success of Chola naval expeditions and the empire's military objectives.

Rajendra Chola's Maritime

Conquests

Rajendra Chola led a series of naval expeditions that showcased the Chola Empire's formidable naval power and strategic acumen. His campaigns were characterized by meticulous planning, audacity, and an unwavering determination to expand Chola dominance beyond the Indian subcontinent.

Under Rajendra Chola's leadership, the Cholas conquered several regions and kingdoms, leaving an indelible mark on the maritime map of the time. These conquests included the subjugation of the Maldives, which strengthened Chola control over key trade routes in the Indian Ocean. Additionally, Rajendra Chola's forces successfully captured Sri Lanka, making it an integral part of the Chola Empire.

Rajendra Chola's audacious expeditions extended further into Southeast Asia. His forces ventured to the region of present-day Malaysia, where they achieved significant victories and established Chola authority over local rulers. Expanding their reach, the Cholas launched expeditions to Sumatra and Java, establishing trade networks, diplomatic relations, and asserting their authority in these distant lands.

The success of Rajendra Chola's maritime conquests can be attributed to the strategic planning and military prowess displayed by the Chola forces. The empire's naval strength, sophisticated warships, and skilled mariners played a crucial role in achieving victory. Rajendra Chola's campaigns were meticulously planned, taking advantage of favorable monsoon winds, knowledge of trade routes, and exploiting the weaknesses of rival kingdoms.

The audacity displayed by Rajendra Chola in venturing beyond familiar shores and conquering distant lands demonstrated his vision of expanding Chola influence. These conquests not only increased the Chola Empire's territorial boundaries but also enhanced its control over vital trade routes, opening up opportunities for economic prosperity and cultural exchanges.

In summary, Rajendra Chola's maritime conquests were marked by strategic planning, audacity, and military prowess. Under his leadership, the Chola Empire expanded its dominance over regions including the Maldives, Sri Lanka, parts of Southeast Asia, and established trade networks in distant lands. These conquests cemented the Cholas' reputation as a dominant maritime power and contributed to the empire's economic prosperity and cultural influence.

Diplomacy and Cultural Exchanges

During his reign, Rajendra Chola recognized the importance of diplomacy and cultural exchanges in maintaining and expanding Chola influence.

Rajendra Chola made significant efforts to establish diplomatic ties with the regions he conquered, recognizing that maintaining peaceful relations was crucial for long-term stability and prosperity. He engaged in diplomatic negotiations with local rulers, offering them favorable terms and incentives to forge alliances and secure their loyalty to the Chola Empire. Through these diplomatic endeavors, Rajendra Chola sought to foster political stability and consolidate Chola control over the regions under his rule.

The Cholas were not only conquerors but also promoters of art, architecture, and religious practices. Rajendra Chola facilitated cultural exchanges between the Chola Empire and the regions it controlled. Chola art and architecture, known for its intricate carvings and grand structures, left a lasting impact on the conquered territories. Temples and monuments built by the Cholas became centers of cultural and religious significance, spreading Chola artistic traditions and religious practices.

Cultural exchanges facilitated by the Cholas resulted in the dissemination of Chola artistic styles, architectural techniques, and religious beliefs. The Chola influence extended to various aspects of life, including sculpture, painting, literature, and dance. The conquered regions were enriched by the introduction of Chola cultural elements, leading to a fusion of local and Chola traditions, which shaped the unique cultural identities of these territories.

The impact of Chola cultural exchanges extended beyond the duration of Chola rule. Even after the decline of the empire, the cultural legacy of the Cholas continued to shape the artistic and architectural traditions of the regions they had influenced. Temples built during the Chola period remained important pilgrimage sites, attracting devotees from far and wide. The Chola impact on local art and architecture endured, becoming an integral part of the cultural fabric of these regions.

Rajendra Chola's diplomatic efforts aimed to establish

peaceful relations with the conquered regions. Cultural exchanges facilitated by the Cholas spread their art, architecture, and religious practices, leaving a lasting impact on the regions under Chola control. The fusion of Chola and local traditions enriched the cultural identities of these territories and continued to shape their artistic and architectural legacy even after the decline of the Chola Empire.

Legacy and Historical Significance

Rajendra Chola's legacy as a visionary ruler and skilled naval strategist is undeniable.

Rajendra Chola's reign marked a significant chapter in the history of the Chola Empire. His visionary leadership and strategic thinking elevated the empire to new heights, solidifying its reputation as a dominant maritime power. His military conquests and diplomatic endeavors expanded the Chola influence, creating a vast empire that stretched across the Indian Ocean region.

Under Rajendra Chola's rule, the Chola Empire became renowned for its naval strength and prowess. The Chola navy, equipped with advanced warships and manned by skilled mariners, was unmatched in the region. The empire's dominance of the seas allowed for extensive maritime trade, cultural exchanges, and the projection of Chola power beyond the Indian subcontinent.

Rajendra Chola's achievements had a profound impact on subsequent Chola rulers and the history of the region. His successes set a precedent for future Chola rulers, who continued to build upon his legacy. The naval strategies and organizational skills developed under his reign provided a strong foundation for the empire's future military endeavors.

The Chola Empire's reputation as a dominant maritime power during Rajendra Chola's reign influenced the geopolitical landscape of the Indian Ocean region. The empire's control over key trade routes and diplomatic alliances brought wealth, stability, and cultural exchanges to the territories under Chola control. The Cholas left a lasting legacy through their architectural marvels, cultural contributions, and administrative systems, which influenced the subsequent history of the region.

In summary, Rajendra Chola's legacy as a visionary ruler and skilled naval strategist is celebrated in history. His reign witnessed the Chola Empire's dominance as a maritime power, facilitating extensive trade, cultural exchanges, and political influence. His achievements laid the groundwork for future Chola rulers and left a lasting impact on the history and culture of the region. Rajendra Chola's contributions continue to be recognized and appreciated as a significant chapter in the rich tapestry of South Indian history.

RAJENDRA CHOLA'S CAMPAIGN AGAINST SRIVIJAYA

Rajendra Chola's campaign against the Srivijaya Empire marks a significant chapter in Chola history, showcasing the empire's military might, strategic vision, and naval dominance.

The Srivijaya Empire, centered in present-day Indonesia, held a dominant position in the maritime trade routes of Southeast Asia during the 11th century. Rajendra Chola, the son of Rajaraja Chola I, ascended to the Chola throne with a deep ambition to expand the empire's influence beyond the Indian subcontinent. To achieve this, he set his sights on the Srivijaya Empire, recognizing the strategic and economic importance of gaining control over its territories and trade networks.

The strategic objectives behind Rajendra Chola's campaign against Srivijaya were multifold. Firstly, he aimed to establish Chola dominance in the lucrative trade routes of Southeast Asia, ensuring that Chola merchants had a stronghold in the region's commerce. Secondly, he sought to neutralize Srivijaya's influence over regional kingdoms and establish Chola suzerainty, thereby extending Chola political control. Additionally, Rajendra Chola aimed to enhance the empire's prestige and reputation as a mighty maritime power by successfully conquering a powerful rival.

The military campaign was meticulously planned and executed by Rajendra Chola. He assembled a formidable naval fleet consisting of warships, auxiliary vessels, and a well-trained force of soldiers. The Chola navy was renowned for its expertise in naval warfare, and Rajendra Chola leveraged this advantage to full effect. The campaign began with the Chola fleet setting sail from the Coromandel Coast, embarking on a long and perilous journey across the Indian Ocean to reach Srivijaya territories.

The Chola forces employed a range of military tactics during the campaign. Their naval dominance enabled them to engage in decisive battles at sea, leveraging superior ship designs, advanced weaponry, and disciplined naval warfare techniques. Boarding maneuvers, naval assaults, and missile attacks were utilized to overwhelm the Srivijaya forces. The Chola navy demonstrated their skill and expertise in maneuvering and coordinating their fleet, which proved instrumental in their victories.

The Cholas' military tactics were supported by strategic planning and resource management. Rajendra Chola ensured that his forces were adequately supplied throughout the campaign, utilizing well-established logistical networks. This enabled the Cholas to maintain their military strength and sustain prolonged engagements.

Through a series of military engagements, the Cholas achieved significant victories over the Srivijaya Empire. They captured key Srivijaya ports and territories, establishing Chola control and influence in the region. The Chola campaign resulted in the subjugation of local rulers, who were made to acknowledge Chola suzerainty. This not only expanded the empire's political reach but also secured a favorable position for Chola merchants in the lucrative trade networks of Southeast Asia.

Rajendra Chola's campaign against the Srivijaya Empire showcased the Cholas' exceptional military prowess, strategic thinking, and organizational skills. The expedition marked a watershed moment in the Chola Empire's history, elevating it to new heights of maritime power and influence. The successful campaign brought immense economic benefits, as the Cholas gained control over crucial trade routes and resources. Furthermore, it solidified the Cholas' reputation as a dominant force in the Indian Ocean region and left a lasting impact on subsequent Chola rulers and the history of the region.

The establishment of Chola maritime outposts played a crucial role in expanding Chola influence beyond the Indian subcontinent. These outposts served as strategic centers for trade, cultural exchange, and political control, enabling the Cholas to exert their influence in distant regions. Let's delve into the details of the establishment of Chola maritime outposts and their subsequent impact:

The Cholas, under the leadership of Rajendra Chola, embarked on a series of successful naval expeditions that resulted in the conquest of various territories in Southeast Asia. With the establishment of their maritime outposts, the Cholas sought to consolidate their control over these conquered regions and facilitate the flourishing of trade and cultural interactions.

The Chola maritime outposts served as bustling centers of commerce, where merchants from different regions congregated to engage in trade. These outposts became hubs for the exchange of goods, ideas, and technologies, leading to the fusion of diverse cultural influences. The Cholas played a pivotal role in facilitating this cultural exchange, bringing their own rich traditions in art, architecture, language, and religious practices to these regions.

Economically, the establishment of Chola maritime outposts led to the growth of trade networks and the expansion of commerce. The Cholas capitalized on their control over key ports and trade routes, effectively monopolizing the trade of valuable commodities such as spices, textiles, precious metals, and luxury goods. The Chola outposts became vibrant economic centers, attracting merchants from neighboring regions and stimulating economic prosperity.

Politically, the Cholas exerted their influence through the establishment of administrative structures and the appointment of local officials to govern these outposts. They introduced their administrative systems, ensuring efficient governance and the collection of revenue. The Cholas maintained a strong military presence in these regions, both to safeguard their interests and to maintain control over the conquered territories.

The cultural, economic, and political influence exerted by the Cholas in these maritime outposts was far-reaching and enduring. The Chola Empire's architectural marvels, such as temples and palaces, left a lasting impact on the regions, showcasing the splendor of Chola art and architecture. The Cholas also spread their religious practices, particularly the worship of deities like Shiva, which became popular in these regions and influenced local religious beliefs and customs.

The economic prosperity brought about by Chola trade and commerce led to the growth of urban centers around the maritime outposts. These centers became melting pots of cultures, attracting people from various backgrounds and contributing to a vibrant cosmopolitan society.

The Cholas' political influence in these regions extended beyond governance and administration. They formed diplomatic alliances with local rulers, fostering political stability and cooperation. The Cholas used their military might and political acumen to forge alliances, negotiate treaties, and solidify their position as dominant regional powers.

The establishment of Chola maritime outposts and the subsequent cultural, economic, and political influence exerted by the Cholas had a profound impact on these regions. It facilitated the exchange of ideas, technologies, and artistic expressions, enriching the cultural landscape. The economic prosperity generated by Chola trade contributed to the growth of urban centers and the development of local economies. Furthermore, the Cholas' political control ensured stability and security, enabling the regions to thrive under Chola influence.

The legacy of Chola maritime outposts can still be witnessed today in the architectural marvels, cultural practices, and historical significance of these regions. The Cholas' cultural, economic, and political influence left an indelible mark, shaping the history and identity of the regions they conquered and establishing the Chola Empire as a powerful force in the Indian Ocean region.

TEMPLE ARCHITECTURE AND ART

The Chola dynasty, known for their remarkable patronage of temple architecture and art, the Cholas left behind a legacy of magnificent structures that continue to captivate and inspire people to this day.

During the Chola era, temples became more than just places of worship; they were architectural marvels and cultural centers that showcased the grandeur and artistic finesse of the dynasty. The Chola rulers displayed a deep reverence for their deities and a profound understanding of the transformative power of architecture and art in expressing devotion.

Under the patronage of the Chola emperors, temple architecture reached unprecedented heights, with each ruler endeavoring to outdo their predecessors in creating awe-inspiring edifices. From intricately carved sculptures to towering gopurams (gateways), Chola temples stood as testaments to the extraordinary craftsmanship and artistic vision of the era.

The Chola dynasty's dedication to temple architecture and art had a profound impact on the cultural landscape of South India. The Cholas created a distinct architectural style known as Dravidian architecture, characterized by its pyramid-shaped towers, richly decorated pillars, and expansive courtyards. Their innovative construction techniques and attention to detail set new standards for temple design, influencing generations of architects and artisans.

The Chola era stands as a golden age for temple architecture and art, showcasing the harmonious blend of religious devotion, cultural expression, and architectural excellence. The temples became not only sacred spaces for worship but also social and cultural hubs, attracting artists, scholars, and devotees from far and wide.

Dravidian Architectural Style

The Dravidian architectural style, synonymous with the grandeur of Chola temples, is a captivating testament to the artistic prowess and visionary genius of the Chola dynasty. Its distinct features and awe-inspiring structures continue to inspire awe and admiration even today.

At the heart of the Dravidian style are the towering pyramidal towers, known as gopurams, that serve as the majestic gateways to the sacred spaces within the temples. These gopurams, adorned with intricate carvings and sculptures, soar towards the heavens, beckoning devotees and visitors alike.

As one enters the temple complex, they are greeted by a vast expanse of spacious courtyards, providing a serene and tranquil atmosphere for spiritual contemplation. The courtyards, often adorned with exquisite stone pillars, stand as silent witnesses to centuries of devotion and artistic brilliance.

Intricately carved sculptures and reliefs adorn every nook and cranny of the temples, depicting scenes from Hindu mythology, celestial beings, and everyday life. The carvings, with their exquisite attention to detail, bring the stories and legends to life, invoking a sense of wonder and reverence.

The Dravidian architectural style, with its emphasis on symmetry, intricate ornamentation, and geometric precision, has had a profound influence on later temple designs in South India. The majestic temples of the Cholas served as an inspiration for generations of architects and craftsmen, shaping the architectural landscape of the region for centuries to come.

To truly appreciate the beauty and significance of the Dravidian architectural style, one must step into the world of Chola temples and witness their grandeur firsthand. Each temple is a masterpiece in its own right, inviting visitors to marvel at the skill and artistry of the Chola craftsmen.

As we delve deeper into the exploration of Chola temple architecture, we will uncover the hidden meanings behind the intricate carvings, discover the spiritual significance of the towering gopurams, and witness the enduring legacy of the Dravidian style in the temples that stand as a testament to the Chola dynasty's artistic brilliance.

Temple Construction Techniques

The temple construction techniques employed by Chola artisans and craftsmen were a testament to their exceptional skill, meticulous craftsmanship, and unwavering devotion to their art. These techniques, honed over generations, resulted in the creation of magnificent temple structures that continue to awe and inspire to this day.

The primary building material used in Chola temple construction was granite, a hard and durable stone. And its strength and longevity made it an ideal choice for creating enduring temple structures. The mastery of stone carving was a hallmark of Chola craftsmanship, as they transformed blocks of granite into architectural wonders.

The process of temple construction was a collaborative effort that involved various skilled individuals. At the core of the construction process was the role of architects, who were responsible for envisioning the temple's design and layout. These architects possessed an in-depth understanding of sacred geometry, proportions, and religious symbolism, allowing them to create harmonious and spiritually significant temple structures.

Sculptors played a crucial role in temple construction, as they meticulously carved intricate sculptures and reliefs that adorned the temple walls, pillars, and doorways. These sculptures depicted deities, celestial beings, and mythological scenes, bringing the temple to life and infusing it with a divine presence.

Artisans, including masons, stonecutters, and craftsmen, worked diligently to transform the architect's vision into reality. They carefully cut and shaped granite blocks, ensuring precision in fitting them together to create the temple's intricate architecture. Each stone was meticulously carved with ornate details, reflecting the artistic excellence and dedication of the craftsmen.

The construction process followed a systematic approach, beginning with the preparation of the foundation, which provided stability and support to the temple structure. The walls were then erected, forming the structural framework of the temple. Intricate carvings, both on the exterior and interior surfaces, were added, showcasing the mastery of Chola stone carving.

As the temple construction progressed, the towering gopurams (gateways) were meticulously built, serving as grand entrances to the temple complex. These gopurams featured elaborate carvings, statues, and multiple tiers, creating a striking visual impact.

Throughout the construction process, religious rituals and ceremonies were conducted to infuse spiritual energy into the temple. These rituals included consecration ceremonies, where the deities were ritually installed, bringing the temple to life and establishing it as a sacred space of worship.

The construction of Chola temples was not merely a physical endeavor but a spiritual journey. It required the harmonious collaboration of architects, sculptors, artisans, and skilled craftsmen who poured their creativity, skill, and devotion into every aspect of the temple's construction. The result was a fusion of architectural brilliance, intricate stone carvings, and a sacred ambiance that continues to captivate and inspire visitors to this day.

Thanjavur Brihadeeswarar Temple

The Temple of Brihadeeswarar, located in Thanjavur, Tamil Nadu, is an architectural marvel and a testament to the grandeur and artistic brilliance of the Chola dynasty. Built during the reign of Rajaraja Chola I in the 11th century, this temple stands as a magnificent example of Dravidian architecture and is a UNESCO World Heritage Site.

The construction process of the Brihadeeswarar Temple was an extraordinary feat of engineering and craftsmanship. It involved the labor of thousands of skilled artisans, architects, and sculptors who dedicated their expertise and creativity to bring this architectural masterpiece to life. The temple was constructed using granite, a material known for its durability and aesthetic appeal. The stones were meticulously carved and interlocked, creating a seamless structure that has withstood the test of time.

One of the most fascinating aspects of the Brihadeeswarar Temple is its massive central tower, also known as the vimana or shikhara. Rising to a height of around 216 feet, it is one of the tallest temple towers in the world at the time. The vimana is a remarkable example of Chola architecture, characterized by its pyramidal shape and intricate carvings. The top of the tower is adorned with a colossal monolithic stone known as the "Kumbam," weighing around 80 tons. The engineering prowess required to raise such a massive stone to such heights is awe-inspiring.

The significance of the Brihadeeswarar Temple for the Cholas cannot be overstated. It served as a center of religious and cultural activities, reflecting the deep spirituality and devotion of the Chola rulers. The temple was dedicated to Lord Shiva, one of the most revered deities in Hinduism. Its construction was not only a symbol of the Chola's devotion to their faith but also a testament to their power and influence.

The temple complex itself is vast and encompasses several structures and courtyards. The main sanctum, housing the lingam, is a sacred space where devotees offer their prayers and seek blessings. Surrounding the sanctum are numerous mandapas or halls, each adorned with intricately carved pillars and sculptures. The temple also features exquisite frescoes and murals depicting scenes from Hindu mythology, adding to its artistic splendor.

Interesting facts about the Brihadeeswarar Temple abound. One fascinating fact is that the temple was constructed entirely without the use of mortar. The stones were meticulously interlocked using an ancient technique. The temple was constructed without digging the earth. Another intriguing aspect is the unique shadow phenomenon that occurs during certain times of the year. The temple's vimana casts no shadow on the ground, creating a surreal and awe-inspiring sight.

The Brihadeeswarar Temple continues to be a living heritage, attracting thousands of visitors from around the world. Its architectural brilliance, spiritual significance, and cultural richness make it a must-visit destination for art enthusiasts, history lovers, and devotees alike. The temple stands as a proud symbol of India's rich cultural heritage and serves as a testament to the architectural genius of the Chola dynasty.

In conclusion, the Brihadeeswarar Temple in Thanjavur is a remarkable architectural marvel and a testament to the Chola's artistic prowess. Its construction process, involving skilled craftsmen and engineers, resulted in a structure that has stood the test of time. The temple's significance to the Cholas as a center of spirituality and cultural expression cannot be overstated. With its towering vimana, intricate carvings, and cultural significance, the Brihadeeswarar Temple continues to inspire awe and admiration, leaving an indelible mark on those who have the privilege of witnessing its grandeur.

Unique Features of Chola Temples

Chola temples are renowned for their unique architectural elements and features that set them apart as remarkable cultural and religious landmarks. These temples exhibit a grandeur and beauty that is truly awe-inspiring.

One of the distinctive features of Chola temples is the towering gopurams, which serve as monumental gateways to the temple complexes. These gopurams are intricately carved and adorned with sculptures, depicting various deities, celestial beings, and mythical creatures. The gopurams not only serve as entrances but also symbolize the spiritual threshold between the mundane world and the divine realm.

Elaborate carvings and sculptures are another prominent feature of Chola temples. The walls of the temples are adorned with intricate artwork, depicting scenes from Hindu mythology, epic stories, and the lives of saints and devotees. The craftsmanship displayed in these carvings is exquisite, showcasing the mastery of Chola artisans in stone sculpting. Every detail, from the expressions on the faces to the flowing garments, is intricately carved, bringing life and vibrancy to the stone.

The layout of Chola temple complexes is carefully designed to create a sacred and harmonious environment. The main sanctum, known as the garbhagriha, houses the principal deity of the temple. It is the innermost chamber where devotees offer their prayers and seek blessings. Surrounding the sanctum are mandapas, or halls, which serve as gathering spaces for devotees and are adorned with elaborate pillars and carvings. These mandapas often feature intricate ceilings with ornate designs and motifs.

Chola temples also often include sacred tanks or water bodies within their complexes. These tanks, known as theppakulams or pushkarinis, hold religious significance and are used for ritualistic bathing and purification purposes. They add a serene and spiritual ambiance to the temple complex, providing a space for devotees to connect with the divine through rituals and contemplation.

The combination of towering gopurams, elaborate carvings, and a well-planned layout creates a unique and immersive experience for visitors to Chola temples. The intricate details and craftsmanship showcased in the carvings and sculptures, along with the sacred aura of the temple complexes, make these structures architectural marvels and symbols of devotion and cultural heritage.

Cultural and Religious Significance

Chola temples hold immense cultural and religious significance, serving as vital centers of worship and spirituality. These temples have been revered for centuries and continue to attract devotees from all corners, establishing a deep connection between people and the divine.

As centers of worship, Chola temples provide a sacred space for devotees to express their devotion and seek blessings from the deities. The main sanctum, with its resplendent idol of the presiding deity, becomes a focal point for prayers, rituals, and spiritual contemplation. The temples are not only places of personal devotion but also facilitate collective worship, fostering a sense of community and shared religious experience.

The Chola rulers played a significant role in promoting the arts, and their patronage led to the creation of exquisite sculptures, paintings, and bronze idols within the temple premises. The intricate carvings and sculptures that adorn the temple walls and pillars are not merely decorative but also serve as embodiments of divine beauty and grace. These artistic expressions evoke a sense of awe and inspire reverence among the devotees.

Chola temples also have a deep connection with the promotion of literature, music, dance, and other art forms. The temples often served as platforms for cultural performances and religious festivals, where poets, musicians, and dancers showcased their talents. The compositions and literary works that emerged from these cultural gatherings have enriched Tamil literature and contributed to the preservation of regional art forms.

Beyond their religious and artistic significance, Chola temples hold a historical and cultural legacy. They stand as testaments to the architectural prowess and aesthetic sensibilities of the Chola dynasty. These temples have witnessed the rise and fall of empires, the ebb and flow of time, and have become living repositories of history and heritage.

In essence, Chola temples embody the synthesis of devotion, art, culture, and spirituality. They serve as spiritual havens where devotees connect with the divine, where art and architecture converge to create an immersive experience, and where the rich cultural heritage of the Chola era is preserved and celebrated.

Devotion and Rituals

Devotion and rituals are integral aspects of Chola temples, creating a vibrant tapestry of religious practices and celebrations. These temples serve as sacred spaces where devotees engage in a variety of devotional acts and participate in time-honored rituals.

On a daily basis, priests perform rituals within the temple premises to offer prayers and invoke the blessings of the deities. These rituals follow a prescribed sequence and are conducted with meticulous attention to detail. The priests dress in traditional attire and perform elaborate ceremonies, including ablutions, offering of flowers and fruits, lighting of lamps, and the chanting of sacred hymns. Devotees gather to witness these rituals and seek the divine grace of the presiding deity.

Chola temples are also renowned for their annual festivals, which are grand affairs that attract large gatherings of devotees from far and wide. These festivals serve as occasions for celebration and religious fervor. Elaborate processions, accompanied by music, dance, and devotional singing, bring the deities out of the sanctum and into the public view. Devotees participate in these processions, offering their prayers and seeking blessings as the divine idols are carried in beautifully adorned chariots or palanquins.

During festivals, the temple complex comes alive with vibrant decorations, colorful lights, and the aroma of flowers and incense. The air is filled with the sounds of religious chants and the rhythmic beats of traditional musical instruments. Devotees immerse themselves in the festive atmosphere, expressing their devotion through prayers, offerings, and acts of charity.

The festivals and processions not only strengthen the bond between the devotees and the deities but also foster a sense of community and shared religious experience. They provide opportunities for devotees to come together, exchange spiritual insights, and deepen their connection with the divine.

Devotion and rituals in Chola temples are not confined to a particular sect or group; they embrace people from various backgrounds and beliefs. The inclusive nature of these practices promotes harmony and unity among the devotees, transcending differences and creating a shared sense of spirituality.

In summary, devotion and rituals form an integral part of Chola temples, providing a platform for devotees to express their love and reverence for the divine. The daily rituals and annual festivals serve as powerful vehicles for spiritual connection and community bonding, reinforcing the deep-rooted religious traditions that have thrived for centuries in the vibrant temples of the Chola era.

Preservation and Restoration

Preservation and restoration play a crucial role in safeguarding the rich cultural heritage of Chola temples. Recognizing their historical and architectural importance, efforts have been made to ensure the preservation and maintenance of these magnificent structures.

Over the years, several organizations, government bodies, and heritage enthusiasts have taken up the task of preserving Chola temples. These initiatives aim to protect the temples from natural decay, environmental factors, and human interventions that may threaten their structural integrity.

Preservation efforts involve a multidisciplinary approach that includes architectural research, documentation, structural assessments, and conservation planning. Skilled professionals, including architects, archaeologists, engineers, and artisans, work together to develop comprehensive strategies for the preservation and restoration of Chola temples.

Conservation projects focus on various aspects, such as stabilizing the foundations, repairing damaged structures, restoring intricate carvings, and ensuring proper drainage and ventilation systems. The use of traditional materials and techniques is often employed to maintain the authenticity and originality of the temples.

Another crucial aspect of preservation is the documentation of Chola temples. Detailed records, including architectural drawings, photographs, and historical documentation, are created to capture the unique features and historical significance of these temples. This documentation serves as a valuable resource for future research, restoration work, and educational purposes.

The ongoing conservation projects are not only aimed at preserving the physical structures but also at promoting awareness and appreciation for the cultural and historical value of Chola temples. Efforts are made to involve local communities, educational institutions, and tourists in these conservation initiatives, fostering a sense of ownership and pride in the heritage.

Preservation and restoration of Chola temples are not limited to individual efforts but also receive support from governmental agencies, non-profit organizations, and international collaborations. These collaborative endeavors ensure a collective approach towards safeguarding and conserving these architectural gems for future generations.

The significance of ongoing conservation projects cannot be overstated. By preserving Chola temples, we not only protect tangible cultural heritage but also ensure the continuation of spiritual practices, artistic traditions, and historical narratives. These temples serve as living testaments to the remarkable craftsmanship, architectural genius, and cultural legacy of the Chola dynasty.

Preservation and restoration efforts are instrumental in safeguarding Chola temples from the ravages of time and other threats. These initiatives not only protect the physical structures but also contribute to the promotion of cultural heritage, education, and tourism. By preserving Chola temples, we honor the legacy of the past and pave the way for future generations to marvel at and appreciate these architectural marvels.

Influence and Legacy

The influence and legacy of Chola temple architecture and art are profound and far-reaching. These architectural masterpieces have left an indelible mark on the cultural and artistic landscape of South India and continue to captivate people from around the world.

Chola temple architecture has been a major source of inspiration for subsequent generations of temple builders in South India. The distinctive Dravidian architectural style, with its towering gopurams, intricate carvings, and spacious courtyards, set the benchmark for temple construction. The design principles and aesthetic sensibilities established during the Chola era continue to shape the architectural identity of temples in the region.

The artistic excellence displayed in Chola temples has had a significant impact on the development of sculpture and iconography in South India. The intricate carvings and sculptures adorning the temple walls depict deities, mythical beings, and intricate motifs, showcasing the exceptional craftsmanship of Chola artisans. This attention to detail and devotion to artistic expression became the hallmark of South Indian temple art.

The legacy of Chola temple architecture extends beyond the boundaries of India. The global recognition of their significance is evident in the designation of Chola temples as UNESCO World Heritage Sites. The temples of Brihadeeswarar in Thanjavur, Airavatesvara in Darasuram, and Gangaikonda Cholapuram are recognized for their outstanding universal value and exceptional cultural significance. These temples attract visitors and scholars from around the world, who marvel at their architectural grandeur and historical importance.

The influence of Chola temples is not limited to the realm of architecture and art. These temples continue to serve as active centers of worship, drawing devotees from various parts of India and beyond. The rituals, festivals, and cultural practices associated with Chola temples have been passed down through generations, maintaining a vibrant religious and cultural heritage.

The enduring legacy of Chola temple architecture and art is a testament to the vision, creativity, and patronage of the Chola rulers. Their dedication to promoting artistic expression, spirituality, and cultural exchange has left an indelible mark on the history of South India. The influence of Chola temples extends beyond their physical structures, as they continue to inspire and engage people with their architectural splendor, artistic brilliance, and spiritual significance.

Chola temple architecture and art have had a profound influence on the cultural, artistic, and religious landscape of South India. The legacy of their architectural style, intricate carvings, and sacred sculptures can be seen in temples across the region. The recognition of Chola temples as UNESCO World Heritage Sites highlights their global significance and enduring impact. The rich cultural heritage and spiritual practices associated with Chola temples continue to be cherished and celebrated, making them an integral part of India's cultural tapestry and a testament to the remarkable achievements of the Chola dynasty.

ADMINISTRATION AND GOVERNANCE

Administrative Structure

The administrative structure of the Chola Empire was known for its decentralized system, where power and responsibilities were divided among different levels of governance. This structure ensured effective management and efficient administration throughout the empire. The Chola Empire was divided into mandalams and each mandalam into valanadus and nadus.

At the local level, the Chola Empire relied on a system of village councils known as Sabhas. These Sabhas played a crucial role in local governance and decision-making. They were composed of elected representatives from the village who were responsible for addressing the needs and concerns of the community. The Sabhas managed local affairs, such as land distribution, irrigation, and the resolution of disputes.

Above the village level, the empire was divided into administrative units called Valanadus. Each Valanadu was governed by a periyanattar and nadu under nattar, who oversaw the administration and governance of the region. They were responsible for maintaining law and order, collecting taxes, and ensuring the welfare of the people in their respective regions.

The kingdom level of governance was headed by the Chola king, who held the highest authority in the empire. The king was supported by a council of ministers and advisors who provided counsel and assistance in the decision-making process. The ministers held key positions in the administration and were responsible for overseeing various departments and functions of the empire.

The decentralized administrative structure allowed for efficient governance and effective management of the vast Chola Empire. It ensured that power was not concentrated in one central authority but distributed among different levels, enabling local concerns to be addressed promptly and efficiently. This structure also allowed for effective communication and coordination between the local administration and the central government.

The division of power and responsibilities at various levels of governance in the Chola Empire ensured that the administration was well-organized and responsive to the needs of the people. It contributed to the stability and prosperity of the empire and allowed for the smooth functioning of the administrative machinery.

Overall, the decentralized administrative structure of the Chola Empire played a crucial role in the effective governance and management of the empire, ensuring that power was distributed, responsibilities were fulfilled, and the welfare of the people was prioritized at all levels of governance.

Village Councils

In the Chola Empire, village councils, known as Sabhas, played a significant role in local governance and decision-making. These Sabhas were integral to the administrative structure of the empire and ensured the active participation of local residents in the governance of their communities.

The Sabhas were composed of elected representatives from the village who were responsible for managing and addressing the needs of the community. The representatives were chosen through a democratic process, where eligible members of the village would elect their representatives based on their capabilities and merit. This system ensured that the voices and concerns of the villagers were heard and considered in the decision-making process.

The primary function of the Sabhas was to manage and oversee various aspects of village life. They were responsible for the distribution of land, allocation of resources, and the maintenance of local infrastructure such as irrigation systems and roads. The Sabhas also played a vital role in resolving disputes within the village and maintaining harmony among its residents.

One of the key aspects of the Sabhas was their emphasis on consensus-based decision-making. Important decisions concerning the village were made through discussions and deliberations among the members of the council. The opinions and viewpoints of the villagers were given due consideration, ensuring a participatory and inclusive approach to governance.

The participation of local residents in the administration of their communities was encouraged and valued in the Chola Empire. The Sabhas provided a platform for the villagers to voice their concerns, offer suggestions, and actively contribute to the development and well-being of their villages. This sense of local ownership and involvement fostered a strong sense of community and collective responsibility.

The Sabhas also served as forums for social and cultural activities within the village. They organized festivals, cultural events, and religious ceremonies, which contributed to the social cohesion and identity of the community. These gatherings provided opportunities for the villagers to come together, strengthen social bonds, and celebrate their shared heritage.

The village councils, or Sabhas, of the Chola Empire exemplified a decentralized approach to governance, where power was distributed among the local communities. The active participation of local residents in decision-making processes ensured that the needs and aspirations of the villagers were given due importance. The Sabhas played a crucial role in managing local affairs, resolving disputes, and fostering a sense of community cohesion. They were a fundamental element of the Chola administrative structure, contributing to the efficient and inclusive governance of the empire.

Bureaucracy

The Chola Empire was known for its efficient bureaucracy, which played a crucial role in the smooth functioning of the kingdom and effective governance. The bureaucracy consisted of a well-organized system of ministers, officials, and administrators who were responsible for various aspects of administration, policy-making, and implementation.

At the top of the bureaucratic hierarchy was the king, who held ultimate authority and made key decisions concerning the empire. The king was supported by a council of ministers, known as the Mantri Parishad or the Royal Council. The ministers were appointed based on their expertise and capabilities in specific areas such as finance, defense, justice, and foreign affairs. They provided advice to the king, implemented policies, and oversaw the functioning of different departments.

The bureaucracy was divided into various departments or ministries, each headed by a high-ranking official. These officials, known as Mahamatra or Mahasandhivigrahika, were responsible for the day-to-day administration and management of their respective departments. They acted as intermediaries between the ministers and lower-level administrators, ensuring smooth coordination and communication.

The administrative system of the Chola Empire was highly decentralized, with a hierarchical structure at the local level. Each region was divided into administrative units known as Mandalams, which were headed by officials called Mandaladhikaris. These officials were responsible for the governance and welfare of their respective regions. They collected taxes, maintained law and order, and implemented the policies and directives of the central government.

Below the Mandaladhikaris were local administrators known as Nadu or Kottam officers. They were responsible for the administration of villages and smaller settlements within the Mandalam. They supervised various aspects of local governance, including land revenue collection, maintaining public order, and resolving disputes.

To ensure effective governance and accountability, the Chola bureaucracy had systems in place for record-keeping and monitoring. The kingdom maintained detailed records of landholdings, revenue collection, and other administrative matters. The bureaucrats were expected to maintain accurate records and provide regular reports to the higher authorities.

The efficient functioning of the Chola bureaucracy was also attributed to the strict code of conduct and ethics followed by the officials. They were expected to uphold principles of honesty, integrity, and impartiality in their work. The system emphasized meritocracy, where appointments and promotions were based on competence and capabilities rather than social status or lineage.

The bureaucracy of the Chola Empire played a vital role in the efficient governance of the kingdom. The ministers, officials, and administrators worked together to implement policies, manage resources, and maintain law and order. Their responsibilities included revenue administration, defense, justice, infrastructure development, and diplomatic relations. The hierarchical structure, systems of accountability, and ethical standards ensured effective governance and contributed to the stability and prosperity of the Chola Empire.

Legal system

The legal system of the Chola Empire was well-developed and played a crucial role in maintaining law and order within the kingdom. The Cholas had a comprehensive system of laws that governed various aspects of society, including civil, criminal, and property matters.

The administration of justice was carried out through a hierarchical structure of courts. At the local level, each village had a council known as the Urar, which was responsible for resolving minor disputes and maintaining order within the community. These village councils had the authority to settle disputes related to land, property, and minor offenses.

For more serious cases, higher courts were established at the district and kingdom levels. The district-level courts, known as Nadu Nattar, were presided over by the district officials and heard cases of greater complexity. These courts were responsible for maintaining law and order in their respective districts.

At the kingdom level, the highest court was known as the Muvendavelar Periya Palai. It was presided over by the king himself or his designated representative. This court dealt with significant criminal cases, appeals from lower courts, and matters of importance to the kingdom.

The judges in the Chola legal system were highly trained and knowledgeable in the law. They were known as

Adhikaris and were appointed based on their expertise and integrity. These judges played a crucial role in interpreting the laws, hearing cases, and delivering judgments.

Disputes were resolved through a combination of oral arguments, examination of evidence, and witness testimonies. The judges relied on legal precedents, established customs, and the prevailing social norms to guide their decision-making process. The Chola legal system emphasized fairness, impartiality, and the principles of natural justice.

The judgments delivered by the courts were enforced by a well-organized system of law enforcement officials. These officials were responsible for ensuring the implementation of court orders, apprehending offenders, and maintaining public order.

Overall, the legal system of the Chola Empire was characterized by its efficiency, fairness, and adherence to established laws and procedures. It played a significant role in maintaining social harmony, protecting the rights of individuals, and upholding justice within the kingdom.

Revenue Administration

The revenue administration system of the Chola Empire was well-organized and played a vital role in sustaining the kingdom's economy. The Cholas implemented a comprehensive system to collect taxes, manage land revenue, and administer other sources of income. The department responsible for land revenue administration in the Chola Empire is called the "Puravuvari-tinaikkalam." The land measurement units used in the Chola Empire include "kuli", "veli", "patti", "padagam", "ma" and more.

One of the primary sources of revenue for the Chola Empire was land taxation. The kingdom had a well-defined system of land measurement and assessment, known as the "ulnagaram." Under this system, the land was classified into different categories based on its fertility and productivity. The revenue officials, known as "Mahattaras," were responsible for assessing and collecting land taxes from the farmers.

Apart from land revenue, the Cholas collected taxes from various sources, including trade, ports, industries, and professions. Taxes were levied on goods transported through ports, and the income generated from these taxes contributed significantly to the kingdom's treasury. The Cholas also imposed taxes on various professions, such as merchants, artisans, and traders.

To ensure transparency and accountability in revenue management, the Chola Empire implemented a meticulous system of record-keeping and auditing. The revenue officials maintained detailed records of landholdings, tax assessments, and collections. These records were periodically audited by higher officials to prevent corruption and ensure that the revenue collection was accurate and fair.

The Chola administration also took measures to prevent tax evasion and fraud. They employed a network of revenue officials who were responsible for monitoring and enforcing tax compliance. They conducted regular inspections and assessments to identify any discrepancies or instances of tax evasion.

To streamline revenue administration, the Cholas

implemented a system of decentralized governance. The revenue officials at the district and local levels had the authority to manage and collect revenue within their respective jurisdictions. This helped in effective management and quick decision-making.

The revenue collected by the Chola Empire was utilized for various purposes, including the maintenance of infrastructure, construction of temples, patronage of the arts, and the welfare of the people. The efficient revenue administration system played a crucial role in the economic prosperity and stability of the Chola Empire.

Overall, the Chola Empire's revenue administration system was characterized by its organization, transparency, and accountability. The meticulous collection and management of revenue ensured the financial stability of the kingdom and facilitated its growth and development.

Role of Chola Kings

The role of Chola kings in the administration and governance of the empire was of utmost importance. As the ultimate authority, the Chola kings held significant power and responsibilities in maintaining law and order, ensuring the smooth functioning of the kingdom, and safeguarding the welfare of their subjects.

The Chola kings were responsible for making crucial decisions regarding governance, including matters of state, diplomacy, and warfare. They formulated policies, enacted laws, and issued decrees to govern the empire. Their wisdom, judgment, and vision played a pivotal role in shaping the course of the Chola Empire.

In addition to their administrative duties, the Chola kings were also the religious and cultural patrons of the empire. They patronized the construction of magnificent temples, supported the arts and literature, and encouraged the practice of religious rituals. Their devotion to the Hindu religion and their patronage of religious institutions added to their authority and influence over the people.

To effectively carry out their responsibilities, the Chola kings relied on a well-structured bureaucracy and a council of ministers. They appointed trusted ministers who held key positions and assisted in governance, providing counsel and expertise in various matters. These ministers played a crucial role in advising the kings, implementing policies, and ensuring efficient administration throughout the empire.

The Chola kings maintained a close connection with their subjects through regular public audiences, where they listened to grievances, resolved disputes, and addressed the concerns of the people. They acted as the ultimate arbiter of justice and were known for their impartiality and fairness in adjudicating disputes.

Furthermore, the Chola kings were responsible for maintaining a strong military and defense system to protect the empire from external threats. They led military campaigns, commanded the army, and strategized to safeguard the borders and expand the empire's territories.

Overall, the role of Chola kings was multi-faceted, encompassing governance, religion, culture, and defense. They played a vital role in the administration of the empire, ensuring stability, prosperity, and the welfare of their subjects. Their leadership and decision-making powers were instrumental in the success and longevity of the Chola Empire.

Ministers and Advisors

Ministers and advisors held significant importance in the Chola administration, playing crucial roles in policy-making, providing counsel to the king, and overseeing the functioning of different departments. They were entrusted with various responsibilities and held key positions in the government hierarchy.

The ministers and advisors in the Chola Empire were chosen based on their experience, wisdom, and expertise in specific fields. They were selected for their administrative capabilities, loyalty to the king, and their ability to provide valuable guidance and advice.

One of the primary roles of the ministers was to assist the king in making important policy decisions. They studied various aspects of governance, assessed the potential impact of policies, and offered their recommendations to the king. Their expertise and insights helped shape the empire's economic, social, and political landscape.

The ministers also had the responsibility of overseeing different departments and ensuring their smooth functioning. Each minister was assigned a specific portfolio, such as finance, justice, trade, agriculture, or defense. They supervised the officials and administrators within their respective departments, monitoring their performance, and ensuring effective governance.

In addition to policy-making and departmental oversight, the ministers acted as advisors and counselors to the king. They provided valuable insights and perspectives on matters of state, diplomacy, and strategy. Their wisdom and experience helped the king in making informed decisions and navigating complex political situations.

The ministers were often part of the king's inner circle and held regular meetings with the monarch to discuss matters of governance. They presented reports, updates, and recommendations, allowing the king to stay informed about the affairs of the empire. The king relied on their counsel and considered their opinions before making important decisions.

The ministers also served as a bridge between the king and the people. They listened to the grievances and concerns of the subjects, ensuring that their voices reached the king's ears. They acted as intermediaries, resolving disputes, addressing grievances, and maintaining harmony within the kingdom.

Overall, the ministers and advisors played a vital role in the Chola administration. Their expertise, counsel, and oversight were essential for effective governance, policy formulation, and the smooth functioning of the empire. Their presence ensured that the king had a strong support system, enabling him to make well-informed decisions and govern the empire efficiently.

Law and order

Law and order in the Chola Empire were of utmost importance, and the kings took several measures to ensure the safety and security of their kingdom. They established a strong military, maintained public safety, and protected trade routes and borders.

The Chola kings recognized the significance of a robust military force in maintaining law and order. They built a formidable army that consisted of well-trained soldiers, cavalry, and a powerful navy. The military was responsible for defending the kingdom from external threats, safeguarding the borders, and protecting trade routes from pirates and other hostile forces.

The Chola kings appointed capable commanders to lead their military forces. These commanders were given the authority to recruit and train soldiers, manage military operations, and maintain discipline within the army. They were also responsible for the defense of strategic locations, such as forts and citadels, which served as strongholds and provided protection to the kingdom.

To ensure public safety within the kingdom, the Chola kings implemented various measures. They established a system of law and justice that was administered by courts and judges. The legal system of the Chola Empire was known for its fairness and efficiency. Disputes were resolved through a well-structured judicial process, which involved the examination of evidence, witness testimonies, and the application of legal principles.

The Chola kings appointed judges who were known for their wisdom, integrity, and impartiality. These judges were responsible for interpreting the laws, delivering judgments, and ensuring justice was served. They played a crucial role in maintaining law and order by settling disputes, punishing criminals, and protecting the rights of the people.

In addition to the judicial system, the Chola kings employed a network of administrative officials and local authorities to maintain law and order. These officials acted as representatives of the king and were responsible for ensuring the enforcement of laws, collecting taxes, and maintaining discipline in their respective regions. They worked closely with the local communities, fostering a sense of accountability and cooperation.

The Chola kings also recognized the importance of protecting trade routes and borders. They took measures to secure the kingdom's frontiers and maintain control over key trade routes, both on land and at sea. They established military outposts, forts, and garrisons along strategic locations to deter potential invasions and safeguard trade.

Trade and commerce played a vital role in the Chola Empire's prosperity, and the kings took steps to protect merchants and traders. They ensured the safety of trade caravans, regulated trade activities, and imposed penalties on those who disrupted or engaged in illegal trade practices.

Overall, the Chola kings were committed to maintaining law and order in their kingdom. Through the establishment of a strong military, the maintenance of public safety, and the protection of trade routes and borders, they created a secure and stable environment for their subjects. These measures not only ensured the safety and well-being of the people but also facilitated the empire's economic growth and prosperity.

TRADE AND DIPLOMACY

Overview of Chola Empire's Flourishing Trade Network

The Chola Empire boasted a flourishing trade network that extended its influence across vast regions. The empire's trade activities reached far and wide, encompassing lucrative commerce routes with diverse regions such as China, Southeast Asia, the Arabian Peninsula, and East Africa.

The Chola Empire's trade network was extensive and well-established, allowing for the exchange of goods and commodities that were highly sought after in different parts of the world. The empire's strategic location along the southeastern coast of India played a vital role in facilitating maritime trade and establishing commercial connections with distant lands.

One of the notable trade routes of the Chola Empire was its engagement with China. Trade relations between the Cholas and China were robust, with significant imports and exports taking place. Chinese goods such as silk, porcelain, and tea were imported into the Chola Empire, while Indian textiles, spices, and other commodities were exported to China. This trade relationship was mutually beneficial and contributed to the economic prosperity of both regions.

The Chola Empire's trade connections also extended to Southeast Asia, where the empire had extensive commerce routes and cultural exchanges. Regions such as Srivijaya, Java, and Sumatra were important trading partners of the Cholas. The Cholas exported textiles, spices, and other valuable goods to Southeast Asia, while also importing commodities like gold, ivory, and aromatic woods. These trade connections fostered economic growth and cultural interactions, with Indian art, architecture, and religious practices leaving a lasting impact on the region.

The Chola Empire's trade network also encompassed the Arabian Peninsula and East Africa. The empire engaged in trade with the Red Sea coast and the Swahili Coast, exchanging commodities like spices, textiles, and precious stones. Indian merchants played a significant role in these trade routes, establishing commercial connections and cultural exchanges with local communities.

The commodities traded by the Chola Empire were diverse and highly valued. The empire was known for its production and export of spices such as pepper, cardamom, and cinnamon, which were in high demand in various regions. Textiles, including fine cotton and silk fabrics, were also a significant part of the trade network. Precious stones like diamonds and emeralds were traded, along with other exotic goods that showcased the empire's prosperity and commercial influence.

The extent and scope of the Chola Empire's trade activities demonstrate its economic prowess and its ability to forge connections with distant lands. The empire's thriving trade network not only contributed to its economic prosperity but also facilitated cultural exchanges, spreading Chola art, architecture, and religious practices to different regions. It is a testament to the Chola Empire's status as a dominant maritime power and its significant role in shaping regional trade and commerce during its time.

Maritime Trade and Connections

The Chola Empire's maritime trade routes played a crucial role in its economic prosperity and cultural exchanges with distant lands. The empire's strategic location along the South Indian coastline provided access to bustling ports and trading hubs, facilitating extensive maritime connections.

The Chola Empire invested significant resources in the development of a robust naval fleet, which was instrumental in expanding and protecting its maritime trade routes. The empire recognized the importance of naval power and maintained a formidable navy that allowed for secure and efficient maritime trade. The Cholas built large, well-equipped warships which is capable of navigating the vast seas and protecting trade routes from pirates and rival powers.

Several ports along the South Indian coastline served as important hubs for maritime trade. Kaveripattinam, also known as Puhar, was one such prominent port that flourished during the Chola period. It was strategically located at the mouth of the Kaveri River, allowing for easy access to inland trade routes and serving as a gateway to Southeast Asia. Kaveripattinam was a bustling center of commerce, attracting merchants from different regions who brought their goods for trade. It played a significant role in facilitating the Chola Empire's trade connections with Southeast Asia and other parts of the world.

Nagapattinam was another crucial port city during the Chola period. Situated on the Coromandel Coast, Nagapattinam served as a vital trading hub, connecting the Chola Empire with various regions in the Indian Ocean. It had strong maritime links with Sri Lanka, Southeast Asia, and the Arabian Peninsula. Nagapattinam attracted foreign merchants and was known for its vibrant commercial activities, including the trade of spices, textiles, and precious stones.

Mamallapuram, also known as Mahabalipuram, was renowned for its seaport and served as a significant center of maritime trade. The port of Mamallapuram was a bustling hub for trade with Southeast Asia, where goods were exchanged and cultural interactions took place. The town was known for its stone carvings and served as a testament to the artistic and architectural excellence of the Chola Empire.

These ports along the South Indian coastline played a vital role in accommodating foreign merchants and facilitating trade. They provided docking facilities, warehouses for storage, and markets where goods could be bought and sold. The Chola Empire encouraged the participation of foreign merchants in its maritime trade, promoting a diverse and vibrant exchange of goods and ideas.

The significance of the Chola Empire's maritime trade and connections cannot be overstated. It brought prosperity to the empire and contributed to its cultural and economic growth. The maritime trade routes fostered cultural exchanges, allowing for the spread of Chola art, architecture, and religious practices to distant lands. They also brought valuable commodities and luxury goods to the Chola Empire, enhancing its wealth and influence in the Indian Ocean trade network. The thriving ports and trading hubs along the South Indian coastline were integral to the success of the Chola Empire's maritime trade and its position as a dominant maritime power during its time.

Trade Relations with China

The trade relations between the Chola Empire and China were significant and mutually beneficial, contributing to the economic growth and cultural exchanges between the two civilizations.

The Chola Empire maintained extensive trade connections with China, particularly during the medieval period. Trade between the two regions flourished, facilitated by maritime routes and a thriving network of ports. Chinese goods, renowned for their quality and craftsmanship, were highly sought after in the Chola Empire, while Indian textiles and spices were in demand in China.

One of the notable imports from China was silk, a luxurious and valuable fabric. Chinese silk was highly regarded for its fine texture and intricate designs. It was used by the Chola royalty and the affluent elite for clothing, decoration, and religious ceremonies. The import of Chinese silk added to the opulence and grandeur of the Chola Empire.

Porcelain, another highly prized Chinese product, was also imported by the Chola Empire. Chinese porcelain was renowned for its delicate craftsmanship and beautiful designs. It was highly valued for its durability and aesthetic appeal. The Chola rulers and the nobility adorned their palaces and temples with exquisite Chinese porcelain, showcasing their wealth and refined taste.

Tea, with its invigorating properties, was another significant import from China. The Chola Empire embraced tea as a popular beverage, and it became an integral part of the Chola society. Tea was consumed by people from different walks of life and became a symbol of social gatherings and hospitality.

In exchange for these Chinese imports, the Chola Empire exported Indian textiles and spices to China. The Indian textiles, particularly cotton fabrics, were renowned for their quality and intricate designs. They were highly valued in the Chinese market and were in demand among the Chinese population.

The Chola Empire also exported various spices to China, including pepper, cardamom, cinnamon, and cloves. These aromatic and flavorful spices from the Chola Empire were prized in China for their culinary and medicinal properties. The spice trade between the Chola Empire and China played a significant role in enhancing the economic prosperity of both regions.

The trade relations between the Chola Empire and China not only brought economic benefits but also facilitated cultural exchanges. The exchange of goods and ideas fostered a deeper understanding and appreciation of each other's culture and traditions. It led to the assimilation of Chinese influences in Chola art, architecture, and lifestyle. Chinese motifs and designs were incorporated into Chola temples and sculptures, showcasing the influence of Chinese aesthetics.

The trade relations with China also contributed to the growth of maritime activities and the development of navigational skills in the Chola Empire. The Chola naval fleet played a crucial role in facilitating this trade, ensuring the safe passage of goods and maintaining maritime security.

The trade relations between the Chola Empire and China were a testament to the empire's economic prowess and its participation in the global trade network. The import of Chinese goods enriched the Chola society, while the export of Indian textiles and spices contributed to the empire's prosperity. The cultural exchanges resulting from this trade relationship added to the diversity and vibrancy of the Chola Empire and left a lasting impact on its history.

Trade Relations with Southeast Asia

The trade relations between the Chola Empire and Southeast Asia, particularly with regions like Srivijaya, Java, and Sumatra, were extensive and mutually beneficial. These trade networks not only facilitated economic exchanges but also led to significant cultural influences and diplomatic ties between the Chola Empire and Southeast Asian regions.

The Chola Empire maintained a strong maritime presence in the Indian Ocean, which allowed for robust trade connections with Southeast Asia. The empire's well-established naval fleet and maritime expertise played a crucial role in facilitating trade and ensuring the safe passage of goods and merchants.

One of the notable aspects of the trade relations between the Chola Empire and Southeast Asia was the exchange of goods and commodities. The Chola Empire exported a variety of products to Southeast Asia, including textiles, spices, precious stones, ivory, and metals. These goods were highly valued in Southeast Asian markets and contributed to the economic prosperity of both regions.

In return, the Chola Empire imported various products from Southeast Asia, such as exotic woods, aromatic resins, rare herbs, and valuable natural resources. The trade with Southeast Asia enriched the Chola Empire with unique and valuable resources that were highly sought after.

Beyond economic exchanges, the trade relations also facilitated significant cultural influences and exchanges between the Chola Empire and Southeast Asian regions. Indian culture, art, and architecture had a profound impact on Southeast Asia during this period. Indian traders, merchants, and artisans brought with them elements of Indian culture, including religious beliefs, rituals, art forms, and architectural styles.

Hinduism and Buddhism, which were prevalent in the Chola Empire, spread to Southeast Asian regions through these trade connections. Temples and shrines dedicated to Hindu deities were constructed in Southeast

THE CHOLA EMPIRE

Asian territories, showcasing the influence of Indian religious practices and beliefs. Indian architectural styles, particularly the Dravidian style, left a lasting impact on the architectural landscape of Southeast Asia.

The spread of Indian culture and religious beliefs was accompanied by cultural exchanges and the assimilation of local traditions with Indian influences. Southeast Asian art and literature were influenced by Indian aesthetics, and Sanskrit became a prominent language in these regions. The blending of Indian and local cultures resulted in the emergence of unique hybrid cultures that have shaped the identity of Southeast Asia to this day.

The trade relations with Southeast Asia also fostered diplomatic ties and political alliances between the Chola Empire and Southeast Asian kingdoms. The exchange of ambassadors, diplomatic missions, and royal gifts helped to strengthen the bonds between the Chola Empire and the rulers of Southeast Asian regions. These diplomatic relations contributed to the stability and mutual cooperation between the Chola Empire and its Southeast Asian counterparts.

In conclusion, the trade relations between the Chola Empire and Southeast Asia were characterized by extensive economic exchanges, cultural influences, and diplomatic ties. The trade networks brought prosperity to both regions, facilitated the spread of Indian culture and religious practices, and led to the emergence of vibrant hybrid cultures in Southeast Asia. The Chola Empire's trade relations with Southeast Asia played a significant role in shaping the history, art, and cultural heritage of both regions.

Trade Relations with the Arabian Peninsula and East Africa

The Chola Empire had significant trade connections with the Arabian Peninsula and East African regions, particularly the Red Sea coast and the Swahili Coast. These trade links played a crucial role in expanding the Chola Empire's influence, fostering economic prosperity, and establishing diplomatic relations with these regions.

The trade relations between the Chola Empire and the Arabian Peninsula were primarily centered around the Red Sea coast. Indian merchants, including those from the Chola Empire, engaged in maritime trade with Arabian traders. The Arabian Peninsula served as an important transit point for goods traveling between India, Africa, and Europe.

One of the key commodities exchanged between the Chola Empire and the Arabian Peninsula was spices. Indian spices, such as pepper, cinnamon, cardamom, and cloves, were highly sought after in the Arabian markets. These valuable spices were used for cooking, preserving food, and medicinal purposes, making them essential trade commodities.

Textiles, particularly fine cotton and silk fabrics, were also prominent trade goods between the Chola Empire and the Arabian Peninsula. Indian textiles were renowned for their quality and craftsmanship, and they found a ready market in the Arabian regions. The Chola Empire's expertise in textile production contributed to the growth of trade in textiles.

Precious stones, including diamonds, rubies, and emeralds, were another significant trade commodity between the Chola Empire and the Arabian Peninsula. The Chola Empire was known for its rich gemstone mines and skilled lapidaries, who cut and polished these precious stones to perfection. The Arabian markets valued these gemstones for their beauty and rarity.

The trade connections with the Arabian Peninsula also facilitated cultural interactions between Indian merchants and local communities. Indian traders brought with them their customs, languages, and religious beliefs, contributing to the cultural diversity of the Arabian regions. The influence of Indian culture, particularly Hinduism, can be seen in the artistic and architectural elements of some historical sites in the Arabian Peninsula.

Moving further east, the Chola Empire had trade links with the Swahili Coast of East Africa. The Swahili Coast was a vibrant trading region where Indian merchants interacted with local Swahili communities. The exchange of goods between the Chola Empire and the Swahili Coast included spices, textiles, ivory, gold, and other valuable commodities.

The trade relations with the Arabian Peninsula and East Africa helped the Chola Empire expand its influence and establish diplomatic relations with these regions. The Chola Empire's economic prowess and its flourishing trade networks made it an important player in the Indian Ocean trade routes. The revenue generated from these trade links contributed to the empire's prosperity and allowed the Chola kings to maintain a strong military and administration.

The diplomatic relations established through trade allowed for cultural exchanges, the exchange of envoys, and the establishment of diplomatic missions. These interactions helped in the formation of alliances, the negotiation of treaties, and the promotion of mutual cooperation between the Chola Empire and the Arabian Peninsula as well as the Swahili Coast.

The Chola Empire's trade relations with the Arabian Peninsula and East Africa were characterized by the exchange of valuable goods, cultural interactions, and the establishment of diplomatic ties. The trade connections expanded the Chola Empire's influence, contributed to its economic prosperity, and fostered cultural diversity in these regions. These trade links played a significant role in shaping the history, economy, and cultural heritage of the Chola Empire and the regions it traded with.

CULTURAL EXCHANGE

During the Chola maritime expeditions, the spread of Hinduism played a significant role in shaping the cultural landscape of the regions they encountered. The Cholas actively promoted the establishment of temples and the propagation of Hindu religious practices and beliefs as they expanded their influence across Southeast Asia and other regions.

One of the primary ways in which Hinduism spread was through the construction of temples. The Chola kings and their armies built magnificent temples in the territories they conquered, serving as religious and cultural centers. These temples not only became places of worship but also played a crucial role in disseminating Hindu teachings and practices to the local population.

The Chola temples were architectural marvels, characterized by their intricate carvings, towering gopurams (gateways), and sacred sculptures. The temples served as a visual representation of Hindu mythology and cosmology, allowing the local population to learn about and engage with Hindu religious narratives. The elaborate rituals and ceremonies conducted at these temples provided opportunities for the local communities to participate and understand the rituals associated with Hinduism.

The Chola kings and their administration also encouraged the patronage of Hindu priests and scholars. These religious figures played a crucial role in spreading Hindu religious beliefs and practices to the local population. They conducted religious ceremonies, taught Hindu scriptures, and provided spiritual guidance to the people.

Furthermore, the Chola Empire facilitated the migration of Brahmins and other religious practitioners to the regions they ruled. These religious experts not only performed religious duties but also acted as cultural ambassadors, disseminating Hindu religious knowledge, customs, and traditions to the local communities.

The spread of Hinduism also led to the assimilation and syncretism of local beliefs and practices with Hindu religious traditions. Local deities and rituals were often incorporated into the Hindu pantheon, leading to the development of unique regional variations of Hinduism in these regions.

The establishment of Chola temples and the propagation of Hinduism had a profound impact on the religious, cultural, and social fabric of the regions influenced by the Chola Empire. Hinduism became a unifying factor, providing a shared cultural and religious identity among diverse communities. The temple complexes served as centers of learning, art, and cultural exchange, fostering a vibrant and dynamic religious and cultural environment.

Even today, the influence of Chola-era Hinduism can be seen in the temples, rituals, and religious practices of the regions once under their rule. The legacy of Chola maritime expeditions in spreading Hinduism continues to shape the cultural landscape and religious practices of these regions.

Language and Literature

The cultural exchanges facilitated by the Chola Empire had a profound impact on the languages and literature of the regions they interacted with. The Cholas, particularly in their interactions with Southeast Asia, played a significant role in spreading the Tamil language and promoting Tamil literature.

The Chola Empire was centered in the Tamil-speaking region of South India, and Tamil was the primary language of the Chola administration and court. As the Cholas expanded their influence through maritime expeditions, the Tamil language and script traveled along with them. This led to the spread and adoption of Tamil scripts in the regions they encountered, particularly in Southeast Asia.

The Chola cultural exchange also involved the translation of Tamil literary works into other languages. Tamil literature, known for its rich poetic tradition and profound philosophical works, captivated the imagination of scholars and intellectuals in the regions influenced by the Cholas. Tamil literary works, such as the epic poems "Silappatikaram" and "Manimekalai," were translated into local languages, ensuring their wider accessibility and influence.

These translations not only preserved the literary heritage

of Tamil but also contributed to the development of literature in the regions they reached. The translation of Tamil texts into languages such as Malay, Javanese, and Khmer resulted in the creation of a new literary tradition that blended Tamil themes and ideas with the local cultural context.

Furthermore, the Chola Empire's cultural exchanges facilitated the exchange of ideas and literary conventions between Tamil literature and the literary traditions of the regions they interacted with. The influence of Tamil literature can be seen in the themes, imagery, and poetic techniques of the literary works produced in these regions.

The spread of the Tamil language and the translation of Tamil literary works into other languages not only contributed to the preservation of Tamil culture but also fostered a sense of cultural connectivity and intellectual exchange between the Chola Empire and the regions it influenced. It promoted multilingualism and cultural diversity, enriching the literary traditions of these regions.

Even today, the impact of Chola cultural exchange on languages and literature can be observed in the surviving texts, inscriptions, and literary traditions of the regions once connected to the Chola Empire. The influence of Tamil language and literature continues to resonate in the languages, scripts, and literary works of these regions, testifying to the enduring legacy of Chola cultural exchange.

Performing Arts and Dance Forms

The Chola Empire had a significant impact on the performing arts, particularly dance and music, and their

THE CHOLA EMPIRE

influence spread to the regions influenced by Chola cultural exchange. Two prominent art forms that flourished during the Chola era were Bharatanatyam dance and Carnatic music.

Bharatanatyam, a classical dance form, originated in the Tamil-speaking region of South India and was nurtured and patronized by the Chola rulers. The Cholas recognized the expressive power and aesthetic beauty of Bharatanatyam and promoted its practice and performance in their courts and temples. As the Cholas expanded their influence through trade and diplomacy, Bharatanatyam also found its way to the regions they encountered.

In the regions influenced by the Chola cultural exchange, local dance traditions assimilated with Bharatanatyam, resulting in the development of unique dance styles and techniques. The fusion of local dance forms with Bharatanatyam led to the emergence of new regional dance traditions that retained the essence of both Chola art forms and local cultural expressions. This assimilation enriched the dance traditions of these regions and contributed to the diversity and vibrancy of the performing arts.

Similarly, the Chola Empire's influence extended to the realm of music, particularly in the development of Carnatic music. Carnatic music, with its intricate melodic patterns and rhythmic structures, found patronage and support from the Chola rulers. The Cholas encouraged the growth of music by establishing music academies and sponsoring musicians and composers.

Through cultural exchange, Carnatic music spread to the regions influenced by the Chola Empire, resulting in the assimilation of local music traditions with Carnatic music. Local musical instruments, melodies, and rhythmic patterns blended with the existing Carnatic music framework, giving rise to distinct regional music styles and genres. This cross-pollination of musical traditions enhanced the richness and diversity of music in these regions.

The assimilation of local dance and music traditions with Chola art forms not only preserved the cultural heritage of the regions but also fostered a spirit of innovation and creativity. It allowed for the exchange of ideas, techniques, and musical compositions, leading to the growth and evolution of performing arts in these regions.

Today, the influence of Chola performing arts can still be seen in the dance and music traditions of the regions once connected to the Chola Empire. Bharatanatyam continues to be a prominent dance form, while Carnatic music remains a vibrant and cherished musical tradition. The legacy of Chola cultural exchange in performing arts serves as a testament to the enduring influence and significance of the Chola Empire in shaping the artistic and cultural landscape of the regions it touched.

Rituals and Festivals

The Chola Empire, known for its rich cultural heritage, had a profound influence on the rituals and festivals of the regions it interacted with during its maritime expeditions. The assimilation and adaptation of Chola rituals and festivals in these regions led to the creation of unique cultural celebrations that blended Chola customs and traditions with local practices.

One of the significant aspects of Chola cultural exchange was the integration of Hindu rituals and festivals. The Chola Empire, being a patron of Hinduism, brought its religious practices to the regions it encountered. The rituals and festivals associated with the worship of Hindu deities, such as Lord Shiva and Goddess Parvati, were introduced and adopted by the local communities.

As Chola customs and traditions merged with the local practices, a syncretic approach emerged, resulting in the creation of unique cultural celebrations. Local customs were intertwined with Chola rituals, leading to the development of distinct regional variations of festivals. These new celebrations retained the core essence of Chola traditions while incorporating local beliefs, folklore, and cultural elements.

For example, the popular festival of Mahashivaratri, dedicated to Lord Shiva, was celebrated with great fervor in Chola territories. This festival, marked by fasting, prayers, and night-long vigils, spread to the regions influenced by Chola cultural exchange. However, the local communities added their own regional flavors and customs to the celebrations, resulting in diverse interpretations of the festival.

Similarly, other Chola festivals such as Panguni Uthiram, Navaratri, and Pongal underwent adaptations and assimilations in the regions touched by Chola cultural exchange. Local communities incorporated their unique rituals, music, dance forms, and culinary traditions, giving rise to vibrant and distinctive cultural celebrations.

The assimilation and adaptation of Chola rituals and

festivals in the regions influenced by their cultural exchange served as a means of cultural preservation and integration. It allowed for the coexistence of diverse traditions and fostered a sense of unity and harmony among different communities.

Today, these cultural celebrations continue to thrive, showcasing the amalgamation of Chola customs with local practices. They serve as a reminder of the enduring legacy of the Chola Empire and its influence on the cultural fabric of the regions it interacted with. The festivals and rituals that emerged from this cultural exchange are a testament to the rich tapestry of traditions and the spirit of cultural unity fostered by the Chola Empire.

Iconography and Sculpture

Chola sculpture and iconography had a profound impact on the regions influenced by their cultural exchange. The Chola Empire, renowned for its exquisite craftsmanship and artistic expression, produced sculptures that reflected their religious beliefs, cultural values, and aesthetic sensibilities. The influence of Chola sculpture and iconography can be observed in the art and sculptures of the regions touched by their cultural exchange.

One of the key aspects of Chola sculpture was the depiction of deities. The Chola Empire, being a patron of Hinduism, produced magnificent sculptures of Hindu gods and goddesses. These sculptures showcased the divinity, grace, and power associated with the deities. The Chola sculptors paid meticulous attention to detail, capturing the nuanced expressions, elaborate ornaments, and iconic attributes of the deities. These sculptures not only served as objects of worship but also as artistic representations of the divine.

The impact of Chola sculpture and iconography extended beyond the representation of deities. Mythical beings, celestial creatures, and cultural symbols also found their place in Chola sculptures. The sculptures depicted various mythological figures and creatures from Hindu mythology, such as Gandharvas, Kinnaras, Nagas, and Yakshas. These sculptures not only showcased the artistic prowess of the Chola craftsmen but also served as visual narratives of mythological stories and legends.

Moreover, Chola sculptures often incorporated cultural symbols that held significance in the Chola Empire. These symbols included royal insignia, sacred emblems, and iconic motifs. The sculptures depicted these symbols with great precision, emphasizing their importance and associating them with the Chola legacy. Such symbols added a distinct identity to the Chola art and made it recognizable across different regions.

The influence of Chola sculpture and iconography in the regions influenced by their cultural exchange was profound. The artistic styles, techniques, and motifs of Chola sculptures were assimilated and adapted by local artists and artisans. These regions embraced the Chola aesthetic, resulting in the creation of sculptures that blended Chola traditions with local artistic sensibilities.

For example, the sculptures in the temples of Southeast Asia, such as Angkor Wat in Cambodia and Prambanan in Indonesia, showcase the influence of Chola sculpture. The depiction of deities, the intricate detailing, and the graceful postures bear resemblance to the Chola style. Similarly, the sculptures in the temples of Odisha and Bengal in India exhibit the fusion of Chola elements with local artistic traditions.

The impact of Chola sculpture and iconography in the regions influenced by their cultural exchange goes beyond artistic expression. It played a significant role in the promotion of Hinduism, the dissemination of mythological stories, and the preservation of cultural heritage. The sculptures served as powerful mediums of religious and cultural symbolism, fostering a sense of connection and reverence among the communities.

Chola sculpture and iconography left an indelible mark on the regions influenced by their cultural exchange. The depiction of deities, mythical beings, and cultural symbols in Chola sculptures influenced the artistic traditions and aesthetics of these regions. The assimilation and adaptation of Chola artistic elements created a unique artistic synthesis, showcasing the harmonious blending of Chola traditions with local artistic sensibilities. Today, the impact of Chola sculpture and iconography can still be witnessed in the magnificent artworks and sculptures that adorn temples and cultural sites across various regions.

Intellectual and Philosophical Exchange

Chola cultural interactions facilitated a significant intellectual and philosophical exchange between Chola scholars and scholars from other regions. These interactions served as platforms for the exchange of ideas, philosophies, and intellectual traditions, leading to a rich intellectual discourse and the mutual enrichment of knowledge.

The Chola Empire, with its thriving centers of learning and patronage of arts and literature, attracted scholars from different parts of the world. These scholars brought with them their own intellectual traditions, philosophies, and scholarly pursuits. They engaged in dialogues, debates, and discussions with Chola scholars, creating a vibrant intellectual atmosphere that fostered the exchange of ideas.

One of the notable aspects of Chola intellectual exchange was the assimilation of various philosophical traditions. Chola scholars embraced different philosophical schools of thought, including Vedanta, Nyaya, Mimamsa, and Buddhism. The Chola Empire became a melting pot of intellectual diversity, where scholars from different philosophical backgrounds engaged in dialogues to explore the complexities of existence, consciousness, ethics, and spirituality.

The exchange of ideas was not limited to philosophical discussions alone. Chola scholars also engaged in the study and interpretation of ancient texts, scriptures, and literary works. They delved into the realms of literature, grammar, linguistics, and aesthetics. This intellectual exchange resulted in the preservation, interpretation, and refinement of ancient texts, ensuring their continuity and relevance.

Furthermore, the Chola Empire served as a hub for the translation of texts from different languages into Tamil and vice versa. Chola scholars played a pivotal role in translating works from Sanskrit, Pali, Prakrit, and other languages into Tamil, making these texts accessible to a wider audience. This linguistic exchange not only facilitated the dissemination of knowledge but also contributed to the development and evolution of Tamil as a scholarly language.

The intellectual and philosophical exchange during Chola cultural interactions had far-reaching impacts. It led to the synthesis and evolution of ideas, the refinement of philosophical doctrines, and the cross-pollination of intellectual traditions. Chola scholars contributed to the growth and expansion of knowledge, enriching the intellectual landscape of the empire and the regions they interacted with.

The impact of Chola intellectual exchange can be seen in the writings, commentaries, and treatises produced during this period. Scholarly works such as the Tirukkural, Tiruvacakam, and the works of renowned scholars like Nammalvar and Manikkavasagar exemplify the intellectual vibrancy of the Chola Empire. These works reflect the profound influence of philosophical, literary, and linguistic exchange on the intellectual pursuits of Chola scholars.

Chola cultural interactions facilitated a robust intellectual and philosophical exchange. Scholars from diverse backgrounds engaged in dialogues, debates, and translations, leading to the assimilation, refinement, and dissemination of ideas, philosophies, and intellectual traditions. The intellectual exchange during the Chola era contributed to the growth of knowledge, the development of new perspectives, and the cultural enrichment of the empire and the regions it interacted with.

Cultural Assimilation and Syncretism

During Chola cultural exchanges, a process of cultural assimilation and syncretism took place, resulting in the merging of local traditions and customs with Chola culture. This process led to the development of unique hybrid cultural expressions that reflected the diversity and richness of the regions influenced by Chola cultural interactions.

Cultural assimilation occurred as a result of the Chola Empire's expansive influence, which encompassed various regions with their distinct traditions, languages, and practices. As the Chola Empire extended its reach, it encountered different cultural communities, each with their own unique customs, rituals, and artistic expressions. Rather than imposing their own culture, the Cholas embraced and incorporated elements of these local traditions into their own cultural fabric.

Syncretism, the blending of different cultural elements, played a crucial role in the process of cultural assimilation. The Cholas and the local communities engaged in a mutual exchange, where they shared their customs, beliefs, and artistic forms. This exchange led to the emergence of hybrid cultural expressions, where Chola influences merged with local practices, resulting in the creation of unique cultural syntheses.

In the realm of religion and spirituality, syncretism was particularly pronounced. The Chola Empire, with its strong patronage of Hinduism, encountered regions with their own religious beliefs and practices. Rather than suppressing these beliefs, the Cholas accommodated and assimilated them into the broader framework of Hinduism. Local deities were incorporated into the pantheon of Chola gods, and local religious practices found their place alongside established Hindu rituals. This syncretic approach resulted in the development of unique regional forms of worship and religious practices.

Art and architecture also underwent a process of assimilation and syncretism during Chola cultural exchanges. Chola temples incorporated architectural styles and motifs from the regions they influenced, resulting in the fusion of diverse architectural elements. Local artistic traditions, such as sculpture, painting, and decorative motifs, merged with the distinct Chola artistic style, giving rise to new artistic expressions that reflected the collective identity of the region.

Language and literature also witnessed assimilation and syncretism. The Cholas promoted the Tamil language and its literary traditions, but they also recognized the importance of regional languages and their literary works. As a result, regional languages and dialects found expression within the broader Tamil literary canon. Translation efforts facilitated the exchange of literary works between different languages, contributing to the development of a rich and diverse literary landscape.

The process of cultural assimilation and syncretism during Chola cultural exchanges resulted in the formation of unique hybrid cultural expressions. These expressions showcased the harmonious coexistence of diverse cultural elements, where Chola influences blended seamlessly with local traditions. The resulting cultural syntheses were vibrant and dynamic, reflecting the shared experiences, values, and aspirations of the Chola Empire and the regions it interacted with.

Chola Empire fostered a process of cultural assimilation and syncretism during its cultural exchanges. The assimilation of local traditions and customs into the broader Chola culture, and the syncretic blending of diverse cultural elements, led to the emergence of unique hybrid cultural expressions. These expressions encompassed religion, art, architecture, language, and literature, showcasing the inclusive and adaptive nature of Chola cultural interactions. The legacy of this cultural syncretism can still be seen today in the diverse cultural traditions and practices of the regions influenced by the Chola Empire.

LEGACY AND IMPACT

The Chola maritime empire, with its grandeur and ambition, etched an indelible mark on the annals of history. Its legacy reverberates through time, evoking a sense of awe and admiration for their profound influence on regional trade, art, and architecture.

In the vast expanse of the Indian Ocean, the Cholas were the masters of the maritime domain. With their mighty ships and unrivaled navigational skills, they charted a course that transcended borders and united distant lands. Their trade networks spanned the horizon, linking vibrant markets from the bustling ports of Southeast Asia to the exotic shores of East Africa.

The Cholas were not mere traders; they were visionaries, catalysts of cultural fusion and artistic splendor. As their ships sailed across the waves, they carried with them treasures that transcended material wealth. Their cargo was a treasure trove of ideas, customs, and beliefs, igniting a kaleidoscope of cultural exchange that would shape the destinies of nations.

Amidst the bustling markets, the aroma of spices mingled with the vibrant colors of textiles, enticing merchants from far and wide. The Cholas, with their keen business acumen, turned trade into an art form, reaping economic prosperity and creating pathways of opportunity. Exotic goods flowed freely, from Chinese silk to Arabian fragrances, enriching the lives of those fortunate enough to partake in this tapestry of trade.

But it was not just material wealth that the Cholas disseminated. They were ambassadors of art, leaving an indelible mark on the canvas of human creativity. Their temples, rising majestically like mountains of devotion, showcased architectural prowess that defied time itself. Every stone, intricately carved and meticulously placed, spoke of a grandeur that surpassed human imagination. The divine figures that adorned these sacred edifices came alive, telling stories of gods and goddesses, of mythical beings and celestial beauty.

And beyond the realms of trade and art, the Cholas were innovators, pioneers of maritime practices that would shape the course of history. Their ships, like floating palaces of adventure, sailed with courage and precision, navigating treacherous waters with unwavering resolve. Their navigational techniques and shipbuilding prowess influenced future generations, becoming a compass guiding the way for maritime civilizations that followed in their wake.

The legacy of the Chola maritime empire continues to captivate our imaginations. It is a testament to the audacity of human endeavor, to the power of cultural exchange, and to the transformative force of trade. The echoes of their footsteps can still be heard, resonating in the bustling markets, inspiring architectural marvels, and shaping the tapestry of human connection across the Indian Ocean region.

As we gaze upon the remnants of their glory, we are reminded of the eternal truth that the impact of a civilization is not measured merely by the monuments it leaves behind, but by the profound transformations it imparts upon the hearts and minds of people. The Chola maritime empire, with its legacy of trade, art, and innovation, continues to stir our souls, urging us to embrace the boundless possibilities that lie beyond the horizon.

The Chola Empire holds immense historical significance and has left a lasting impact on the cultural and architectural landscape of South India. Known for its administrative excellence, maritime prowess, and patronage of the arts, the Chola dynasty flourished between the 9th and 13th centuries CE. The empire reached its zenith under rulers like Rajaraja Chola I and Rajendra Chola I.

One of the most iconic and revered architectural masterpieces of the Chola Empire is the Brihadeeswarar Temple, located in Thanjavur, Tamil Nadu. This temple, dedicated to Lord Shiva, is a testament to the architectural brilliance and artistic achievements of the Chola dynasty. Its construction was initiated by Rajaraja Chola I in the 11th century CE.

The Brihadeeswarar Temple is renowned for its towering vimana (temple tower), which stands at a height of around 66 meters and is one of the tallest temple towers in the world. The temple complex also includes a large central courtyard, intricately carved pillars, mandapas (halls), and a massive stone bull known as Nandi. The walls of the temple are adorned with exquisite sculptures and carvings, depicting deities, celestial beings, mythical creatures, and intricate motifs.

The Brihadeeswarar Temple, along with other Chola temples, has been recognized by UNESCO as a World Heritage Site. This prestigious designation acknowledges the outstanding universal value and significance of these temples as cultural and architectural treasures. The Chola temples represent a remarkable fusion of artistic creativity, technical skill, and religious devotion.

The global recognition of Chola temples highlights their architectural grandeur, artistic excellence, and the cultural legacy of the Chola Empire. These temples serve as a testament to the rich cultural heritage of South India and attract visitors from around the world, including art enthusiasts, historians, and spiritual seekers.

The UNESCO recognition also brings attention to the need for their preservation and conservation. Efforts are made to protect and restore these architectural marvels to ensure their longevity and safeguard them for future generations. These temples continue to inspire and awe with their grandeur, intricate craftsmanship, and spiritual significance, serving as a bridge between the past and the present.

In the vast expanse of history, the Chola maritime empire emerges as a mesmerizing chapter that continues to captivate our imagination. Their legacy, deeply interwoven with the fabric of seafaring and trade, has left an indelible mark on the world, shaping the course of regional trade, art, and architecture in ways that still echo today.

The Cholas, with their intrepid spirit, embarked on ambitious maritime expeditions that stretched across the vast Indian Ocean. With their sturdy ships and unparalleled navigational skills, they ventured into uncharted waters, pushing the boundaries of human exploration and discovery. Their seafaring prowess became the stuff of legends, as they navigated treacherous seas and established lucrative trade networks with distant lands.

Their influence on regional trade was nothing short of transformative. The Chola maritime empire opened up new avenues for commerce, connecting diverse cultures and fostering economic prosperity. Their ships carried a treasure trove of goods, from exquisite textiles and aromatic spices to precious gemstones and exotic treasures. Through these maritime trade routes, the Cholas facilitated the exchange of goods, ideas, and cultural practices, creating a vibrant tapestry of cross-cultural influences.

But their impact extended beyond trade alone. The Cholas were true innovators, pushing the boundaries of maritime technology and navigation. They developed sophisticated shipbuilding techniques, crafting vessels capable of withstanding the perils of the open sea. Their navigational prowess, aided by astrolabes and celestial charts, allowed them to traverse vast distances with remarkable accuracy. These advancements in maritime practices laid the foundation for future seafaring civilizations, influencing the development of navigation techniques across the

Indian Ocean region.

The Cholas' architectural and artistic contributions also left an indelible imprint on the landscapes they encountered. Their temples, resplendent with intricate carvings and majestic sculptures, stand as testaments to their artistic mastery. The Chola architectural style, characterized by towering gopurams, intricate stone carvings, and elaborate mandapas, inspired generations of builders and architects. These architectural marvels, such as the Brihadeeswarar Temple in Thanjavur, continue to awe and inspire visitors from around the world.

As we gaze upon the legacy of the Chola maritime empire, we recognize its enduring impact on the world today. Their influence on regional trade, art, and architecture transcends time, reminding us of the transformative power of cultural exchange. The Cholas' legacy serves as a beacon of inspiration, urging us to explore the uncharted, embrace diversity, and forge connections that transcend borders.

In the annals of history, the Chola maritime empire shines as a testament to the audacity of human ambition and the thirst for knowledge. Their legacy beckons us to chart our own course, to sail beyond the known horizons, and to celebrate the beauty of cultural assimilation. The Cholas have bequeathed us a remarkable inheritance, a rich tapestry of maritime heritage that continues to shape the world we inhabit.

REFERENCES

Sastri, K. A. Nilakanta. (2002). The Cholas. Chennai: University of Madras.

Gai, G. S. (2003). The Chola Empire. New Delhi: National Book Trust.

Keay, John. (2001). India: A History. New York: Grove Press.

ABOUT THE AUTHOR

Parthasarathy G

Parthasarathy G, an Engineering Graduate from Tamilnadu, India, brings together his diverse experiences in the IT industry and his deep passion for humanities, life, and social sciences. With a career spanning over a decade, he has delved into the intricate workings of society, philosophy, and motivation.

Residing in Chennai, the vibrant capital city of Tamilnadu, Parthasarathy G is surrounded by the rich cultural heritage of South India, which serves as a constant inspiration for his writings. His books are a reflection of his profound understanding of human life, the pursuit of a better society, and the exploration of philosophical concepts.

In his latest work, "The Chola Empire: Legends of the Indian Ocean," Parthasarathy G takes readers on an awe-inspiring journey through the golden age of the Chola Empire. Immerse yourself in the captivating tales of maritime adventures, cultural exchanges, and architectural marvels that shaped the history of the Indian Ocean region.

Connect with Parthasarathy G on social media to stay

updated on his latest publications, behind-the-scenes insights, and engaging discussions:

Instagram: @parthapages
Twitter: @sarathy1210

Join the conversation and embark on a voyage through time and knowledge with Parthasarathy G's thought-provoking works.

Printed in Great Britain
by Amazon

f493b6a7-977a-4431-bac0-284a96c37091R01